TRIPLE MY LISTINGS

27 Marketing Ideas for
FREE SELLER LEADS

KNOLLY WILLIAMS

Introduction

Hi there!

I am extremely excited and honored that you have decided to read *Triple My Listings*.

For more than a decade, I have spoken around the world to real estate agents eager to succeed at the highest levels.

I put this book together at the request of my Mentorship Masters members. Mentorship Masters is my FREE Mentorship Program for real estate agents, and my members have been asking me for my most treasured ways to generate Listing Leads.

Mind you I have 5 complete chapters focused on Lead Generation in my book *Success with Listings*, however I don't delve too deeply into my specific tactics there.

Thousands of agents have read and implemented *Success with Listings* to GROW their real estate practice, and now they are ready to generate a boatload of fresh listings.

This book will help you do just that.

Are you looking to generate more Listing Leads?

Do you want to finally have a steady pipeline of business with sellers practically begging you to list their house?

Well in this book I've compiled my 27 most effective and favorite ideas for helping you generate a non-stop supply of Seller Listing Leads.

These are the same ideas I trusted to list more than 1,000 homes during my first 10 years in the business.

The cool thing is you don't have to implement them all! Just implement a handful of these ideas and generate all the listing business you can handle.

After you've begun implementing these ideas, you may find that you would like to reach out to me directly, so that I can personally help you succeed.

If so, consider joining my FREE Mentorship Masters program.

When you join my FREE Mentorship Masters program (a group I run through eXp Realty), you become a member of my family, and I become obligated to Your Ultimate Success!

Find out more about Mentorship Masters and join at PartnerWithKnolly.com

Now then, onward to YOUR Success!

Read through this book of Ideas and pick the ones that resonate with YOU!

If it's not your cup of tea, move on to the next idea! Pick 3 or 4 ideas and get off to the races!

To Your Success,

Knolly Williams

Bestselling Author & International Speaker

P.S. I also included some great video training that will accompany some of the key concepts you learn in this book. You can simply scan the QR Code next to the videos you want to watch, or go to Knolly.com/FreeTMLVideos to watch them all! Enjoy!

NOW YOU CAN...

✓ Exponentially Grow Your Business While Working Less

✓ Avoid Hundreds of Hours of Costly Mistakes Doing the Wrong Things

✓ Generate More Income than You Ever Thought Possible

✓ Avoid the Hustle and Create Success Faster and Easier

✓ Earn 6 Figures, Take Nights and Weekends Off and Be Debt Free

✓ Generate All the Listing Leads You Want

Developing the Daily Lead Generation Habit

What is the first and foremost important activity of a successful Listing Specialist? Of course you already know the answer: *lead generation.*

In ancient times, our forefathers were hunter-gatherers. Back then, people migrated with their food source and hunting for the next meal was not an *optional* exercise.

No matter how scarce the surrounding food supply seemed, our ancestors would relentlessly chase their prey until they achieved success. For them, failure meant starvation and death. So when the food supply was abundant, they stockpiled and carefully preserved and stored the surplus. In good times and bad times they never took their eye off the ball.

If you want to be successful, you are not at liberty to treat lead generation like an optional exercise. Lead Generation is the ONE activity which allows all the other aspects of your career to become a reality. Prospecting is the cornerstone of your career.

When you take on a new listing, what is the ultimate goal you are hoping to achieve for your client? *A successful sale.*

What is the ultimate goal you are hoping to achieve for yourself? *A paycheck and a client for life.*

In order to receive a paycheck, you have to have a closing. In order to have a closing, you have to have a contract. In order to have a contract, you have to have an offer. In order to have an offer, you have to have a listing. In order to have a listing, you have to have a client. In order to have a client, you have to prospect. In order to have a prospect, you have to lead generate. Lead Generation is the catalyst that burgeons into paychecks.

TIME BLOCK FOR SUCCESS

A successful Listing Specialist will conduct their lead generation activities in the morning hours, typically before noon.

9 AM to 11 AM (or Noon) is a pretty typical time block for lead generation. Generally speaking, 2 to 3 hours a day, Monday through Friday is preferable.

Handling your lead generation in the morning hours, when you are at your peak performance and maximum energy level is the way to go.

In order to achieve success with your lead generation activities, you will need to block out your daily lead gen time in your calendar.

Set it there as a hard and fast daily appointment, and don't break the routine.

THE 4 STAGE LEAD LIFECYCLE

In real estate all leads have what I call a four stage lead lifecycle. This is true not only for real estate, but for any area of sales.

Most agents speak about and focus on just one stage in this process, *lead generation*. In fact, this is only the *first* step in what is a four-step process. Generating leads without capturing, incubating and converting (lead follow-up) will not necessarily lead to clients. Those who focus merely on stage one will miss many a payday.

In order to be achieve Success with Listings you absolutely have to take most seller leads through the entire 4 Stage Lead Lifecycle. Stages 2 through 4 are the stages that determine if a lead will live (and reward you monetarily along with the possibility of repeat business) or die (and reward you with nothing).

Stage 1: LEAD GENERATE

Stage 2: LEAD CAPTURE

Stage 3: LEAD INCUBATE

Stage 4: LEAD CONVERT

Stage 1: Lead Generate

We call this *Lead Generation*. This is the step where the hook is baited and you are 'fishing' for leads. Lead Generation involves marketing and promotion, and a variety of other tactics required to generate a lead.

Stage 2: Lead Capture

We call this *Lead Capturing* or *Lead Receiving*. This is the stage where the lead actually falls into your hand and you catch (or capture) it. During this stage you have the lead captured, but it is uncertain whether or not this lead will actually turn into a *paycheck* for you. Hard work and diligence is required in order to take the lead all the way to the pay window.

Stage 3: Lead Incubate

This is what I call the 'nurturing' stage. As my mentor Rand Smith says, *"In order for someone to work with you, the possibility of trust has to exist."*

Think of this as the step where you are getting the lead to trust you. You are nursing the lead and trying to get them to see that working *with* you is a better choice than working *without* you. You are working to show them that you can be trusted.

Sometimes the lead incubation process is quite lengthy. Other times, (depending on the lead source, your skill level and contact frequency) it happens very naturally and quickly.

Step 4. Lead Convert.

Leads that are converted have graduated to become *clients*. In order to take a lead all the way to step 4, you absolutely have to *connect* with them. What I mean is, a connection between you and them has to have taken place.

It is unfortunate that many real estate agents completely drop the ball when it comes to stages 2 and 3. Many of the Type A personalities (High Ds on the DISC profile) that I train try to take a lead from Stage 1 directly to stage 4. They want to generate the lead and immediately convert them. If the lead doesn't convert right away, they move on to the next one. Don't make this mistake. Stages 2 and 3 are where the magic happens. If you want to build your listing business to the highest level it can possibly be, you will have to get good and consistent at capturing and incubating your seller leads. You can easily double your business just by making sure your leads are captured and incubated. These leads can often turn into clients, months down the road. If you do not focus on these critical stages, then many of your potential listings (and paychecks) will simply fall through the cracks.

You'll be happy to know that you can delegate steps 2-4 to your team members if they are highly trained and skilled at converting leads (yes, it truly is an art form). You can also make use of drip email campaigns and other systems to help you capture and incubate your leads.

HANDLING OBJECTIONS

Oftentimes listing agents completely fumble the ball when a seller prospect throws out an objection. I have witnessed an agent's energy change and I have watched them go on the defensive when objections are raised.

While the agent may attempt to mask their emotions, this subtle change from positive to neutral or negative energy is immediately picked up by the prospect, and defeat is imminent if the agent cannot recover quickly.

As you move toward mastery in the lead generation game, you will continue to encounter objections, yet the more skilled you become, the easier these objections will be to navigate through.

What Is An Objection?

Think of some words that you would consider being synonymous with the word *objection*. What comes to mind? Typically we think of objections as *obstacles*.

What I want you to realize is that *an objection is not rejection.* An objection is an *opportunity*.

Let's say for example that you are talking to a prospect about listing their property and they throw out an objection such as *"I like what you have to offer, but I haven't seen your signs in our neighborhood"* or *"Your fees seem higher than the other agents that I've talked to"* or *"What makes you think you can sell my house when my previous agent couldn't?"* With these questions, what is the prospect really saying? I believe they are saying *"Knolly, I think you can probably sell my house and I want to list with you. Can you please confirm for me that I am making the right decision?"*

Remember, an objection is not rejection. An objection is an opportunity. If the prospect did not want to explore the idea of listing with you they would not throw out an objection in the first place.

Think about the way you make big decisions. Before you swipe the card on that $400 purse, a flood of questions races through your mind. *"What's your return policy?" "When did you say the newer designs are coming in?" "What if I find it for less somewhere else?"*

Why do you get this barrage of questions right before you make a big decision?

The reason is that we are programmed to not want to make a big mistake. We throw up objections to protect ourselves. We want confirmation that we are making the right decision before we fully commit. We may also want to know where the escape hatch is (or whether or not there is one) before we jump on board. Once our objections are handled, we can feel safer about moving forward.

As a Listing Specialist, when you handle objections effectively you are reaffirming to the prospect that they are making the right decision by hiring you to list their house.

If the prospect did not want to list with you in the first place they wouldn't have any objections. Instead of asking questions they would simply tell you that they are not interested.

Again think of when you were pitched a product to purchase. If you were not interested you would simply tell the salesperson "no, thank you" and move on. You wouldn't stand there and began asking questions about the product unless you were considering the idea of buying it.

In order to handle objections masterfully, you need to master the material in this book and learn your scripts backwards and forwards.

WHY AGENTS DON'T PROSPECT

There is a wide array of excuses that real estate agents provide for why they do not prospect regularly. No excuse is warranted or valid. Lead Generation is a daily activity.

Lead Generation is critical to your success. Next I would like to address some of the most common excuses that I've heard for not prospecting. Let's examine them together.

Excuse #1: *"I'm so busy! I just can't seem to find the time!"*

Imagine our forefathers waking up and thinking *"I've got a lot of things to do today, so I guess I won't go out hunting. Feeding my family can wait."*

In our businesses we can easily become distracted by that which is *urgent* and forget about that which is truly *important*. Everyone and everything may seem to be vying for your attention, but nothing deserves it more than your lead generation time.

No matter how busy your world gets or how much business you currently have in your pipeline, you should never take your foot off the lead generation pedal. Your time block for lead generation should be anchored to your schedule and honored daily.

Excuse #2: *"I've tried to time-block but I keep getting distracted."*

Allowing yourself to become distracted means that you are not correctly protecting your time block period. Be sure that everyone in your family and your office understands the importance of this activity. In ancient times, nothing was more important than hunting. This still holds true today. Imagine a family member discouraging the patriarch from going on the daily hunt, because of some other matter.

Purposely protect your lead generation space by hanging a note on the door that says "LEAD GENERATING. PLEASE DO NOT DISTURB." Close the door if you can. Also, take any snacks, coffee, water and other supplies with you into your lead generation bunker. Even the distraction of leaving your desk to fetch a drink of water or a coffee refill may prove fatal. If you are less than supremely disciplined when taking short breaks, then you should be anchored to your desk until you have achieved your goal for the day (lead generate for 3 hours, make 20 contacts, set 2 appointments, etc.).

Excuse #3: *"I just can't get in the habit of time blocking."*

You absolutely can get into the habit of time blocking because you already time block now. In fact, you have learned to time block since the day you were born.

Do you go to sleep every night? That's a time blocked activity. Do you brush your teeth, shower and get dressed every morning? Each of those is a time blocked activity. Do you eat meals every day? That's a time blocked activity. When you worked a 9-to-5 job, did you go to the movies during your work hours? Of course not, because you time blocked 8 hours for work and did personal activities during your off work hours!

Even when you go to the movies you are time blocking 2-3 hours of undisturbed time.

You already know how to time block and you do it every day. If you are not time blocking for lead generation in your real estate practice, then you have not yet come to realize the correlation between prospecting and paychecks.

- Prospecting = Paychecks
- Not Prospecting = Poverty

Excuse #4: *"I don't know what to say."*

Knowing what to say is critical and oftentimes we fail to lead generate because we are afraid that we either don't know what to say or we will say the wrong thing.

Knowing what to say is a matter of training and learning your scripts. As you master the material and learn the scripts in this book, you will know exactly what to say to your prospects.

Excuse #5. *"I don't know what to do."*

You've time blocked your schedule and plopped yourself down at your desk promptly at 9 AM. Now what? Obviously, knowing what to do during your lead generation time is very important.

For a Listing Specialist, lead generation is the activity of generating new seller leads.

During your lead gen time, you should be:

1. Prospecting for new seller leads (lead generation).
2. Following up on your existing leads (lead incubation).
3. Implementing marketing plans.

OVERCOMING THE FEAR OF PROSPECTING

Some agents are actually afraid to lead generate, because they fear rejection.

You can greatly reduce or eradicate this fear by coming to realize this one simple truth: *It's Not About You*. Yep – it sounds like a cliché, yet it is so true at so many levels.

Working with a seller is first and foremost about helping a person in need. You are helping someone else achieve success. Firstly you are adding value to them. Coincidentally you are receiving value in return.

For example, let's pretend you are a master roofer. You decide to go on a 2 week mission trip to a remote village to help the villagers restore their roofs, which are in terrible disrepair. You hop on a plane and take a grueling 13 hour flight. Then, after a 2 hour bumpy and dusty jeep ride through a remote and unnamed road, you arrive at your destination.

Now then, what do these villagers need? A new roof. Why are you there? To put as many new roofs on as you can over the next 2 weeks. Are you confident that you can do the job? Of course! You are a master roofer.

The only question that remains is – *will the villagers allow you to help them to get what they need?*

What if some of the villagers don't allow you to help them? Perhaps a foreigner has done them wrong in the past, or they just grew up with the notion of not trusting others. You show up with your sleeves rolled up and tools in tow. You knock on the door and your interpreter explains why you are there. The villager looks at you and smiles, but shakes his head *"NO."* The interpreter pleads with him, as it is clearly obvious that his roof is one of the worst in the village and it is leaking badly. Unfortunately the villager remains suspicious, rejects your act of kindness and ultimately shuts the door in your face.

You feel rejected.

But ask yourself, was this rejection about you or is it about them? Of course, it's about them. It has nothing to do with you because you are eminently qualified to achieve success for them. If this villager had allowed you to, you could have placed a gorgeous new roof on their hut within four hours. You have no choice but to move on to the next house. Luckily for them, they are not so resistant. After a bit of conversation through the interpreter, they follow you around the outside of their hut as you point out what you are going to do for them. They invite you in with open arms. They even celebrate their new roof and thank you by preparing you a delicious local dish.

Your Prospects Have to Be Willing to Allow You to Help Them.

When you are rejected by a prospect it is usually not about you, it's about them. People come to us with a boatload of past experiences, trust issues, and the like. Our job is to help them overcome their fear, apprehension and trust issues so that we can help them get what they want. You will use your skills, your scripts, your tools, and your notoriety simply as leverage to help your prospects make the right decision to hire you for the job of selling their house. Once they hire you, you can confidently move forward to help them achieve success.

As Listing Specialists, we must let go of ego. We must become servants who are singularly focused on knowing what our clients want and need, so that we can serve it up to them.

On the other hand, if they choose not to hire you don't take it personally and don't be offended. It's okay. It wasn't meant to be. Place them in your incubation system and move on to the next one.

If someone does not allow you to help them to succeed it is not about you it's about them. Likewise, when someone does hire you, it is still not about *you* it is about them. Understanding and internalizing this simple truth will help you overcome your fear of rejection and your fear of prospecting. Shake it off and move on.

Of course you should have 100% confidence in yourself, knowing that you are the best person for the job. You should always be improving yourself, your skills, your tools, your systems and your tactics.

WHERE WILL YOUR LEADS COME FROM?

Becoming a top Listing Specialist requires a nonstop supply of listing leads. As it turns out – there are only three sources that all the leads you will ever need will come from. I call these the 3 Lead Generation Buckets.

As you go through my list of the Top 27 Ideas you will see that they each fit neatly into one of these lead buckets.

I am convinced that the reason most agents do not realize their highest success potential in the real estate game is because 1) they are not primarily focused on listings, 2) they do not have the right leverage and 3) they are not consistency generating leads during their lead gen time, through the 27 Ideas outlined in this book.

It may help to think about the three lead generation buckets as the three legs of a stool. Suppose you wanted to stand on a heavy duty 3-legged stool (you know, the tripod style). It will support and distribute your weight quite nicely. What would happen though if you took one of those legs off and tried to stand on it? The stool simply would not support you. What if you took two of the legs off?

You would end up flat on your back.

Sadly most real estate agents are trying to stand on a one legged stool – and that one leg that they do have is busted and in disrepair.

The 3 Lead Buckets (the 3 legs of your stool) are:

1. **SOI** (your sphere of influence).

2. **Farm** (your geographic farm).

3. **Niche** (your specialty).

From these 3 buckets you will generate all of the leads that you will ever need.

In this book I will help you tap into these 3 lead buckets by implementing a handful of the Top 27 Ideas I cover.

But first let's take a look at *Why Agents Fail.*

Why Agents Fail

According to Forbes magazine, 80% of businesses fail.

Unfortunately, statistics for the real estate profession are even more dismal.

NAR reported that 87% of all new agents fail within five years in the industry and only 13% make it.

A business where nearly 9 out of 10 people who enter fail would appear to be a *very risky business indeed*.

But why do agents fail?

I absolutely love studying success. It's probably my favorite topic of all to read about.

Success always leaves clues.

I also like to study about failure so that I can avoid costly mistakes for myself and my Mentorship Masters students.

After studying success for more than 30 years I have come to realize that the recipe for success is actually quite simple.

To be successful… all you have to do is study and learn about what other successful people are doing and just do what they have done.

We might call it *Success Hacking*.

When it comes to success in your real estate practice, there is no reason for you to reinvent the wheel.

The power of having a mentor is absolutely undeniable.

Because real estate is considered a very competitive industry, most of the top real estate agents in your market will not feel comfortable sharing their best success secrets with you.

Why would they want to train up the competition? They have a mindset of *"there isn't enough to go around"*.

That's why I created Mentorship Masters, my FREE Mentorship Program for real estate agents. Our members have direct access to my complete coaching program at NO CHARGE.

In fact, I wrote this entire book because several of my Mentorship Masters members asked me specifically how I was able to take more than 100 listings a year for more than 10 years in a row… <u>WITHOUT EVER HAVING TO PAY FOR LEADS</u>.

At Mentorship Masters we are all about helping each other succeed. We don't embrace the concept of *"lack"* and we believe that there is more than enough to go around.

Just 8 months after I got my real estate license I hired my first coach. I paid $1,000.00 a month and I was in my rookie year!

But I was determined to be a success.

My coach helped me go from a goal of 40 deals per year to more than 100. And within my first 10 years I sold more than 1000 homes.

This would never have happened for me without a good coach and mentor.

One of the primary reasons that I created Mentorship Masters was to ensure that my members are a success.

I know that many agents don't have a spare $1,000.00 a month laying around to allocate toward coaching, yet I also know that they could realize their highest hopes and dreams *if they only had the right mentorship*.

While many agents put their hopes squarely on technology and training, I believe that *mentorship* is the golden key to your success.

When Jesus was upon the earth he was in the business of *discipleship*. He did this to show us a model for how to build up successful leaders.

He spent three years teaching his disciples *everything* that he knew. The *Jesus Model* has become the standard that we use at Mentorship Masters.

We know for a fact that it is impossible to fail when you align yourself with successful people and you put in the work that is required of you.

Do you sincerely believe that?

The reason that 87% of agents fail in the business is because they don't have a successful role model that can take their hand and show them exactly what to do, what to say and how to say it.

They are floundering on their own *without a mentor*.

For my Mentorship Masters Members, things are very different.

It's a program where you are surrounded by people who care about you, who love you and who are eager to see you successful.

Your Ultimate Greatness

If you are new in the business or just looking to reboot your real estate game, we are going to ensure that you do not fail like the other 87%. We are going to mentor you so that you can soar to your highest possible heights.

If you are already a successful agent and/or run a team, we are here to mentor you and to challenge you to even higher heights. We are also here to support your agents.

If you run a team, let me help coach your team members to their ultimate potential, so you can invest your time in generating more leads using the ideas outlined in this book.

If you are a solo agent, I am here to coach you to <u>YOUR ULTIMATE GREATNESS</u>.

We want you to succeed at the highest levels of your capability – with the least amount of effort.

So, whether you are looking to *learn the ropes* or you desire to scale up your business to new heights, Mentorship Masters is the program designed with YOU in mind.

The Program is Absolutely FREE for Agents who partner with me.

TAKE A LOOK AT WHAT YOU GET WHEN YOU JOIN MENTORSHIP MASTERS TODAY:

1. Membership in the Mentorship Masters SUCCESS PORTAL

2. Mentorship Masters Weekly Group Coaching Call

3. Kevin & Fred Bi-Weekly Group Coaching Call

4. Full Day Private VIP Retreats with Knolly and other leaders

5. FREE Access to ALL of Knolly's Tools and Systems

<u>Check out my complete Mentorship Masters Program at PartnerWithKnolly.com TODAY.</u>

Now it's time for us to dive into some of the ideas that will help you **GET MORE LISTINGS NOW...**

Chapter Homework

Watch Knolly's FREE Videos for this Chapter to help you grow your success even faster! To watch simply go to
Knolly.com/FreeTMLVideos
or scan the QR Code Below of the video you want to watch.

Videos Included for this Chapter:

☐ **Why Agents Don't Prospect!**

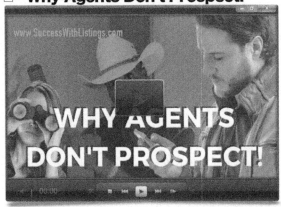

☐ **How to Get Listing Leads! (without cold calling)**

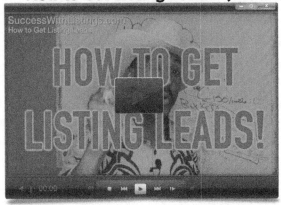

☐ How to Dominate the Listings Game: Success with Listings LIVE Event

☐ Getting Started with Lead Generation (Real Estate Lead Gen Secrets Part 1 of 12)

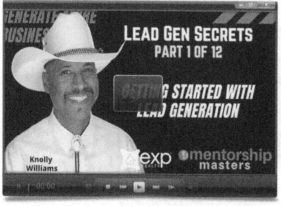

☐ **The Psychology Behind Successful Lead Generation (Real Estate Lead Gen Secrets Part 2 of 12)**

☐ **Setting Yourself up for SUCCESS - MORE LISTINGS NOW - (Real Estate Lead Gen Secrets Part 3 of 12)**

☐ Generating More Leads in Your Real Estate Business

IDEA #1:
Communicate with Your SOI (via Email) Every Single Month

Your Sphere of Influence (SOI) is your most critical lead generation source. This will understandably be your largest and most important target market when it comes to generating an untold fortune in the real estate game.

Retaining a current client is more important than generating a new one. You have already invested a great deal of time and energy cultivating the relationship you have with these folks, and they already command your loyalty.

Unfortunately, a great many real estate agents spend vast sums of money, time, attention and energy trying to generate new relationships while completely abandoning their current ones. If you orphan your clients your competitors are waiting in line to adopt them.

Keeping in touch with your SOI is critical! Your SOI is made up of past clients, people you know and people you've met.

According to a recent survey conducted by the National Association of REALTORS® (NAR), when selecting an agent to sell their house 7 out of 10 sellers chose their agent based on a referral by a friend, neighbor or relative, or they used their previous agent.

That means 70% of your business will come from or originate from someone in your database. This is what we call repeat and referral business.

Another survey conducted by the NAR revealed that 84% of sellers say they are likely to use the same agent or recommend that agent to others.

That means 84% of your past clients would refer you or reuse you! That's not bad. Yet how many people actually do reuse the same agent again or refer them to their SOI?

Shockingly, the research points to just 9%-11% of them. This is a remarkable disconnect. Why is it that nearly 90% of the folks who say they would refer you or use you again never do? The answer is obvious.

You are not staying in touch with them.

Based on the aforementioned statistics, 70% of your income should come from your SOI. Now let's convert this data into a little math exercise. Let's say that your goal is to net $100,000 this year.

Let's further pretend that you were adequately marketing to your SOI on a consistent basis. According to the data,

$70,000 of the $100,000 income you earn over the next twelve months will come from this one bucket alone. However, if you do not stay in touch with your SOI, them this bucket dwindles down to right around $9,000. Ouch.

Let me explain it another way. When it comes to eating out, many people base their decision to try out a new restaurant on the restaurant's star rating. If a restaurant has 4.5 out of 5 stars (based on numerous patron reviews), would you eat there? Absolutely. Would you eat at a restaurant that received 1 out of 5 stars (with numerous patron reviews)? Not likely.

That establishment would likely be on their way *out of business*. The research shows that when you abandon your sphere of influence, your rating drops from 4.5 stars to a 0.5 star! That's a half a star rating! Ouch.

So the question is WHY AREN'T YOU STAYING IN TOUCH WITH YOUR SOI???

Think about the question.

What is your excuse?

Why are you willing to give up so much of your potential income?

Throughout my career as a trainer I've heard a variety of excuses as to why agents are willing to forgo the vast sums of wealth that should be continually springing forth from their database.

If 70% of your business will come from your SOI wouldn't it make sense to spend most of your lead generation time, attention, effort and marketing budget on this group?

Of course!

Yet most agents seem obsessively and obstinately focused on following every new scheme, tactic, and strategy that comes along promising to deliver fresh new leads. In other words, they choose to spend the majority of their time focusing on and marketing to *complete strangers* while ignoring those who already know, like and trust them. Such thinking is foolish and should be abandoned immediately.

It is so important to communicate with your SOI via email on a monthly basis.

For my monthly contact to my SOI, I use a monthly email Newsletter from MoreSolds.com. MoreSolds is a CRM (Client Relationship Manager) that I created several years ago for my team. We wanted a system that was robust and feature rich, yet easy to use, so we created our own. We now make our CRM available for free to anyone who wants to use it.

Setting up an email newsletter takes less than 5 and then it's automated and works for you month after month, keeping you in touch with your sphere.

Too many agents get caught up in manually piecing together articles, and when the monthly chore of compiling a customized newsletter becomes too time-consuming, they abandon doing it altogether.

Your primary focus is on touching your clients each and every month. The articles should be made up of short and relevant content.

The beauty of MoreSolds is that our E-Newsletter editor researches what is trending that month and includes shortened versions of those articles. They handle all of the back end work so you don't have to.

Plus it is automatically customized with your photo, logo, contact information, *Featured Listings* link, *Property Search* link and more, so it looks like YOU created it.

Remember, if you rely on doing this manually, it oftentimes won't get done.

Research the various systems available and pick the one you love. Regardless of what program you use to send out your email newsletter, it should be *'set it and forget it'* simple. In other words, you want to use a system that you can set up once and your newsletter will automatically go out each and every month, like clockwork.

Chapter Homework

Watch Knolly's FREE Video for this Chapter to help you grow your success even faster! To watch simply go to
Knolly.com/FreeTMLVideos
or scan the QR Code Below to watch.

Video Included for this Chapter:

☐ **Your Real Estate Database - An easy plan for staying in touch with your SOI**

☐ **Visit MoreSolds.com for more info on sending out your Monthly Newsletter**

IDEA #2:
Communicate with Your SOI via Postal Mail Every Quarter

Each quarter, mail a jumbo sized (5 1/2" x 8 1/2" or similar size) postcard out to your database.

Rather than sending a new postcard each quarter, simply print up a batch and send the same one every three months.

For example, if your database is 250 people, you would simply print 1000 postcards and send that same postcard every three months.

If you try to change up the design of your postcard every three months, you will invariably discontinue the campaign because you simply won't get around to getting the job done.

Remember – your goal is simplicity. Yes, you could create a new postcard every quarter but that is completely unnecessary. Again, the point of the mailing is to tap your SOI on the shoulder and remind them that you are still in business and that you still *need* business. Make it easy on yourself by printing up one batch of postcards and using that same one throughout the year.

Your postcard should double as an *item of value* (IOV). My favorite for shelf life is a Preferred Vendor Directory. You could also consider including the following:

- Friends and family discount coupon (i.e. $500 off your next transaction);
- Referral Reward (i.e. $50 Visa gift card);
- Free House Valuation;
- Free copy of your book (a free printed copy of your seller book; see Idea #14).

Print & Assign

When it comes to delivering your postcards, simply have them printed and assign the job of mailing them to your Admin. If you don't yet have an Admin, you can entrust the job to your kiddos, a neighborhood student, or anyone else willing to help.

When the mailing is due, simply drops off the box of cards, addresses labels and postage stamps, and have the person get your mail-out ready and sent.

Delegating this helps you automate the process while you stay focused on the most dollar productive activities.

Mailing for FREE

Did you know you can get the cost of your printing and mailing paid for by your Preferred Vendors?

Now let's suppose your database is 400 people. Mailing to your farm would cost just under $200 in postage. Printing the flyers would run about. Printing would cost about $100. That's a total of $300

All you need to do is invite four service providers to participate in your mailer. Each trade will receive a small ad on the back of your postcard and they each invest just $75.

Now how much will it cost to you to mail your marketing piece? *Nothing.*

Local trade vendors make good candidates. For $75 they can piggyback on your mailer and reach 400 folks who know, like and trust you! You can also include more than 4 trades and bring the price down further for each participant.

IDEA #3:
Call Your SOI at Least
Twice a Year

Twice a year you will want to pick up the phone and call your SOI. Again this is solely for the purpose of continuing to stay in touch with them.

You can easily spread those calls out evenly throughout the year. For example, let's say you have a database of 300 people. This means that you will make 50 phone calls each month, or 12 calls each week.

It should take you no more than forty minutes to a few hours to make those 12 calls.

Considering that you should be time blocking for lead generation at least 2-3 hours each day, these calls are both wonderful and profitable, and can easily be incorporated into your lead generation time.

You: Hi Penny its _____ - how are you?

SOI: Great! it's good to hear from you. We are doing well, how are you doing?

You: I'm doing awesome, Penny. Hey Penny, the reason I'm calling is just to touch base and see how things are going. The last time we talked your daughter Suzy had just gotten a new puppy and your son Charles was about to graduate from high school.

SOI: [talks about what's new while you take notes about what's new in their life and enter these notes into your CRM]

You: Penny – thanks again for taking the time to catch me up on what's going on with you guys! Right now my business is doing well but I still have a big problem that I was hoping you could help me with.

SOI: Sure... What's up?

You: Penny, my biggest problem right now is with our inventory. Our listings are selling fast and we need more! I'm looking to help 2 more families to buy or sell before the end of the month. Who do you know that's thinking about buying or selling?

SOI: hmmm... You know... no one comes to mind right now.

You: Thanks Penny. I really appreciate your help. As always Penny, if you happen to overhear anyone talking about selling - let them know that you'd love to have your agent give them a call with some free advice. Then just text me, email me or better yet, CALL ME with their contact info. Can you do that for me?

SOI: I sure will!

You: Thanks again Penny! By the way - I'm also going to be sending you a few copies of my new book... it's a complete Seller's Guide that you can pass along to anyone you run into that's thinking about selling.

SOI: Wow, that's great!

You: Thanks again Penny - you have a great day!

SOI: You too!

Follow Up Email:

Hi Penny,

It was so great talking with you today. Thanks again for your time.

I was delighted to hear about how Roxanne is going off to college and about your job promotion! Congrats to you and Steve on both accounts! [Here you are inserting a sentence or two about your phone conversation/highlights of what you discussed]

Like I mentioned, if you come across anyone who is thinking about selling or buying (even if they are just tossing around the idea), I would love to help!

I have found that it's best if you just get me their name and phone number so I can follow up with them. CALL ME with their information and I promised to give them the same level of service I provide to all my close friends and family. You can always email me their info or text me if that's more convenient.

I am looking forward to helping 2 more families buy or sell before the end of the month, and I look forward to your help!

Thanks again Penny!

Enter the Call Notes into Your CRM

It is important that you enter your notes about the call into each client's contact record on your CRM. You know how your doctor pulls out a clipboard at your annual physical and briefly discusses your medical history that you discussed with her the year before?

Clients love it when you can briefly restate what you discussed on the last call with them. When they see that you were paying attention to what is going on in their life, they will become all the more loyal and will want to strongly support you.

You may also find it helpful to visit their Facebook and LinkedIn page, so you can catch up on what's going on with them just before you make the call.

IDEA #4:
Make an Introductory Call to Your SOI to Reestablish TOMA

One of the best ways to clean up your database and reacquaint yourself with your SOI is with an *introductory call* to reestablish TOMA (Top of Mind Awareness).

If you are like most agents, chances are your database is a little outdated.

You will need to go through your database with a fine-toothed comb and update all of your contacts while adding any new ones you have written down. This will require some research and phone calls to your existing database.

Here's a sample call script to folks you haven't talked to in a while:

Script!

You: Hi John! It's _____ with _____. I sold your home a few years ago.

SOI: Oh - Hi!

You: You know John, it's been a while since we've talked. Frankly, I apologize for not being in touch with you.

SOI: Oh, I understand.

You: Thanks John. You know from this day forward I've decided to commit myself to staying in touch. My goal is to call you about every six months, just to see how you, Jill and the family are doing. Would that be okay?

SOI: Sure!

You: Awesome! Well let me just make sure that I have all your current information. Is your home address still 301 N. Hickory Cove?

SOI: Yep

You: Awesome. And is this the best number for you?

SOI: Yep

You: Great. What's your current email address?

[Keep going along these lines until you have updated all of their contact information]

You: Thanks again John! As I mentioned, I'll be contacting you about every six months just to see how you guys are doing. Plus Penny - I have a pretty large database with folks in almost every profession you can think of, so let me know if you ever run across anyone looking for a job, or if you need a good handyman, painter, roofer, electrician, attorney or whatever!

SOI: Great! I sure will.

You: Awesome! Oh - one more thing John. My biggest problem right now is with our inventory. Our listings are selling fast and we need more! Who do you know that's thinking about selling?

SOI: hmmm... You know... no one comes to mind right now.

You: Thanks John. I really appreciate your help. As always John, if you happen to overhear anyone talking about selling - let them know that you'd love to have your agent give them a call with some free advice. Then just text me, email me or better yet, CALL ME with their contact info. Can you do that for me?

SOI: I sure will!

You: Thanks John! By the way - I'm also going to be sending you a few copies of my new book... it's a complete Seller's Guide that you can pass along to anyone you run into that's thinking about selling.

SOI: Wow, that's great!

You: Thanks again John – you have a great day!

SOI: You too!

After your call be sure to send a follow-up email using your version of my previously discussed follow up email script.

Once your database is squeaky clean, it will stay that way by implementing the strategies you are learning in the book.

Developing and maintaining your SOI is the best way to reach optimal success in the real estate business.

Your database will consistently reward you with repeat and referral business when you consistently stay in touch with them.

IDEA #5:
Recruit Your Top 25 Contacts to Generate Leads for You

Now that we have thoroughly examined a few ideas for consistently reaching your SOI, I want you to consider creating your own *inner circle*. An inner circle can make big things happen in your listing business.

Having an inner circle is another Biblical principle. In his ministry, Jesus had thousands of disciples, yet he hand-picked just twelve to be part of his inner circle.

Your inner circle will be the cream of the crop, hand selected from your SOI.

Did you realize that you could effectively do 100 real estate transactions a year from an inner circle group of just 25 people?

You could if those 25 individuals were highly connected people that would each commit to sending you just one referral each quarter.

Your inner circle will be individuals who you can count on for multiple referrals each year. You will want to stay in contact with this group more frequently, and perhaps have a periodic client appreciation parties/events just for them.

ANCHORING YOUR GOALS INTO A HIGHER PURPOSE

Personally, I am very big on the concept of paying it forward and giving back. I would love to see you anchor your real estate goals into a higher purpose.

I believe that our mission in life should be tied to a higher purpose. I'm convinced that my duty on earth is to serve God and others. That's what leadership is per Jesus' own example.

Imagine if you took a little from each commission check you earn to help a needy cause.

One example is helping to put wells into villages that don't have safe and potable water.

Another friend I know spent years raising money to build incredibly nice mini-houses (huts) for villagers who spent the majority if their lives living in cardboard boxes situated on a land fill. These little huts were some of the cutest you've ever seen and cost only about $5,000 each.

What my wife Josie and I personally do is we have the title company where we close our transactions wire 10% of our funds from every closing directly into a "ministry" account. It's a separate account and we call it *God's Account*. Although we realize that the biblical practice of tithing is no longer a mandate, we still love and follow the principle as it is always a good practice to pay it forward.

We use the money in God's account to fund missionaries, feed the poor, help those who fall on bad times, assist widows and orphans (for anything outside of ourselves). This is not something we have ever shared publicly because we don't do it for publicity.

We are absolutely sure that we get more benefit from giving than those who are the recipients.

We just personally feel compelled to pay if forward - and we have been allocating 10% of our income for more than 20 years. We do it from a spirit of gratitude and thankfulness. We started doing this in 1992 and we have never stopped. Back then we were both making less than $7 an hour and our monthly household income was less than $2,000 with both of us working full time jobs! It was tough to do, but the Lord has always blessed us with an abundance and taught us to fully trust in His provision.

Let's look at an example of how anchoring your purpose into a higher calling works.

Let's say for example, that Cynthia is a busy Listing Specialist. She is committed to reaching her goals and she is also committed to giving back. Cynthia does the research and finds out that for $3,000, she can fund a well for a village in a third world country. Just one well would provide clean and safe drinking water to more than 300 villagers, greatly reducing infection and disease in that area.

Now let's say Cynthia has a goal to list 40 houses this year. She decides to donate $300 from each closing to her "well" project.

This means that for every 10 houses that Cynthia closes, she can provide funding for one well. Therefore, once she reaches her closings goal for the year, she would have also reached her higher goal of providing fresh drinking water for four villages.

Cynthia's goal is now firmly anchored into a higher purpose. Instead of having a goal to sell 40 houses, her goal this year is to put in four wells.

As Cynthia is calling on her SOI to solicit listing referrals – instead of asking past clients to help her reach her goal of selling 40 houses this year, she can ask them to help her reach her goal of providing safe drinking water to 4 villages.

For every client that her inner circle refers her, they are actually helping make the world a better place. Meanwhile they are making Cynthia's world better too. It's a win-win.

Cynthia: Hi Jim, it's Cynthia over at the Baker Team. How are you?

Jim: Oh, Hi Cynthia – we are doing well, how about you?

Cynthia: Awesome Jim. Hey – I'm calling because we have a wonderful new project that I wanted to let you know about, so you can help me spread the word.

Jim: Great, what's up?

Cynthia: You know Jim - My team and I found out that people in Haiti are literally dying because they don't have access to fresh drinking water. We also found out that we could put a well into a village that would provide clean and safe drinking water for over 300 people, and save lives. Our team is going to cover all the costs; we just need your help getting the word out. Does that sound like something you could help with?

Jim: Sure! How can I help?

Cynthia: Well Jim, our goal is to put in 4 wells this year that will serve over 1200 people. Basically for every house we close this year we are donating a portion of the proceeds to this project. For every 10 properties we close we can fund a well.

Jim: Cool!

Cynthia: So Jim, all we need you to do is send us the contact information of anyone you run across that is thinking about buying or selling. Every referral you send us will go toward helping with our big goal of putting wells into these villages! Doesn't that sound great?

Jim: You bet!

Cynthia: Thanks Jim. I knew we could count on you. I'm going to be keeping track of our goal and keeping you updated periodically. By the way - how many referrals do you think you can send me over the next 12 months?

Jim: Well... I don't know - maybe five.

Cynthia: That's great Jim - I'll put you down for five. I'll also email you some more for information about this incredible project! Thanks again Jim!

Jim: You bet Cynthia!

Using the script above, all Cynthia would have to do is keep contacting her sphere of influence. If she contacted 20 inner circle contacts and each person made a commitment of 2-3 people, she can count on 40-60 referral leads this year from this target group!

In order for the program to be a success, Cynthia will have to hold those who made pledges accountable. She will do this by writing down each person's commitment and then tracking it on a spreadsheet. Each quarter she can send out a spreadsheet showing exactly where things stand. Her quarterly report can show the names of those who pledged referrals, the number of referrals that they pledged, the actual number of referrals that they have sent (year to date), and the referrals remaining to be sent. The report would also show how many wells have been put in and how many there are to go. She can follow up her quarterly report with a phone call thanking those who are making good on their pledges and encouraging the ones who have not.

Your clients love to get behind a project that is for the good of others. That's why anchoring your goals into a higher purpose can help you achieve what you want faster. Now then, if Cynthia were simply to call her sphere of influence without a higher purpose goal, her message would not have the same affect.

Imagine Cynthia just calling her database and letting them know that her goal was to increase her wealth by selling 40 houses this year, or simply to help 40 families buy or sell. This doesn't have the same ring. Her sphere of influence can feel much more motivated to help her reach an altruistic goal of serving 4 villages.

There are literally hundreds of different things you could do to pay it forward both domestic and abroad. Just pick one.

You could provide scholarships, help kids pay for summer camp, fund art classes or music lessons, provide wheelchairs for the elderly, home restorations for veterans, fund self-improvement classes, help rescue animals... the list goes on and on. Pick something that is near and dear to your heart, figure up the cost, factor how much you are willing to donate (percentage or fixed amount) from each closing and go to work getting your SOI on board with your higher purpose!

In doing so you will be a blessing to others, allow your SOI an opportunity to pay it forward, and provide for your family.

You should think about this as a "project" and run it as such, on an annual basis.

Here's an example of a project to provide wheelchairs for the elderly:

1. **Project Purpose**: Provide wheelchairs for the elderly.

2. **You closings goal**: 60.

3. **Cost per wheelchair:** $400.

4. **Amount you decide to donate from each closing**: $100.

5. **12 Month Project Goal:** Provide 15 wheelchairs for the elderly.

With this example, your unit goal is 60 closed units over the next 12 months. You find out that you can purchase rehabbed wheelchairs for around $400 each, and you decide to donate $100 of each closing toward the project. Once you reach your unit goal, you will have provided 15 wheelchairs for the elderly.

That's $100 per closing x 60 closings = $6,000 ÷ $400 (cost of each wheelchair) = 15 wheelchairs.

Let's say you need 100 referrals in order to project 60 closings. Your group of 20 people will need to commit to sending you an average of 5 referrals per person. If your inner circle is 40 people, you would only need 2.5 referrals a year from each person.

As you can see, anchoring your goals into a higher purpose is a wonderful way to achieve your goals while simultaneously making the world a better place.

Chapter Homework

Watch Knolly's FREE Videos for this Chapter to help you grow your
success even faster! To watch simply go to
Knolly.com/FreeTMLVideos
or scan the QR Code Below of the video you want to watch.

Videos Included for this Chapter:

☐ **Recruiting Your SOI to Generate LEADS for
YOU (Real Estate Lead Gen Secrets Part 5 of
12)**

☐ Become a TOP AGENT TODAY! (PART 1 of 2)

IDEA #6: Build a Geographic Farm

A geographic farm is in area of town that you specifically target with the express purpose of becoming well known in that territory.

Although your geographic farm probably won't be as large as your sphere of influence, over time it can grow to create a substantial portion of your income.

Success at geographic farming requires having an action plan, a budget, being creative, doing some hard work, and being realistic in your expectations.

Most top agents that are seasoned have a geographic farm they work with, and many have been working those areas for years.

Let's look at some criteria to consider when putting your farm together.

500+ Houses

A good farm will be made up of at least 500 houses. Ultimately, the size of your farm will depend on your sales goals. I know some agents who have a farm of 10,000 or more houses. My suggestion is to start with around 500 houses and increase the size of your farm over time.

Area Should Have Steady Turnover/Sales (7% Minimum)

The area you choose to farm should have a minimum sales turnover of 7%.

For example, suppose you pick a farm area with 500 houses. Using the 7% turnover rule, at least 35 houses per year should sell within your farm each 12 months (500 x 7%).

You should be able to use your local tax record data to determine the actual number of houses in an area or subdivision. Then, to determine how many houses are actually selling in your target area, you can do an MLS *"Sold"* report to see how many houses actually sold there in the past 365 days.

If you are having trouble coming up with these reports, your team leader, coach or broker should be able to help you.

The Average Sale Price Should Be Enough to Support Your Goals

One of the most obvious ways to increase your income is to increase your average sale price. Farming is one of the easiest ways that I know of to increase your average sale price, because you get to *choose* which neighborhoods and areas you want to work in.

Keep in mind that it costs the same to market to high-end neighborhoods as it does to low income areas.

At any rate, you will want to make sure that the areas you target are at least within your acceptable average sale price goals.

"How Long Will it Take to Begin Seeing Results?"

Farming takes time. Just like creating success in other areas of life, it boils down to time on the task over time. If you are effectively marketing to your farm utilizing all of the strategies in this chapter, it can take several months to begin seeing steady results.

Achieving success with farming is a commitment. Success has a lot to do with the activities you are doing, and sticking with the program. If you are not seeing the results you want, then more than likely you are not doing everything I've discussed in this chapter, you are not giving the program long enough to succeed or you have unrealistic expectations.

SETTING REALISTIC EXPECTATIONS

Oftentimes agents give up on farming when they don't see the results that they expect very quickly. Again, Success with Listings is about time on the task over time. It's also about having realistic expectations.

You should aim for a goal of having a 20% listing market share in your farm area. I've seen agents grow to a 50%+ market share in their target area, but 20% is a realistic, doable and worthy goal.

What that means is that if there are a total of 40 property sales a year in your farm area, your goal will be to eventually grow your market share in that area to the point where you are listing 20% of the houses that sell there annually. In this case success would mean that at least 8 of those 40 sales are your listings.

For some this number may seem low but eight sold listings is nothing to sneeze at. For example if your gross commission is $9,000 from each of those listings, then your GCI from this strategy alone will be $72,000. That's a great return on investment considering that you don't have to spend much more than a few hours a day a few days a week sowing in that field. If your goal is to sell 20 houses, then all you would have to do is increase the number of houses that you market to by broadening your territory.

Chapter Homework

Watch Knolly's FREE Videos for this Chapter to help you grow your success even faster! To watch simply go to
Knolly.com/FreeTMLVideos
or scan the QR Code Below of the video you want to watch.

Videos Included for this Chapter:

☐ **Getting Started with Geographic Farming - Real Estate Lead Gen Secrets Part 6 of 12**

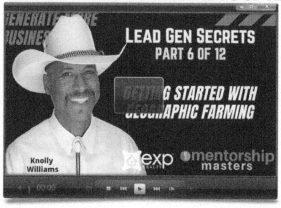

☐ More Listings through Farming (for Real Estate Agents)

IDEA #7:
Canvas Your Target Areas on Foot

Yes, this is old fashioned door knocking!

Get out and walk the neighborhood that you farm at least once a month. You can hit as many as 100 homes in a three hour time block.

Have an Item of Value (IOV).

Hand the homeowner something of value. If they aren't home, you can leave it at the door.

Your IOV can be a newsletter with valuable coupons, a calendar of events, a sports schedule, neighborhood sales statistics or a vendor trade directory.

The main idea in canvassing your area is to simply be seen in and around the neighborhood.

As folks begin seeing your face along with your other marketing materials and strategies which you were doing in the area (Idea #6, 8, 9, 10 and 11) you will be reinforcing that you are the agent of choice for that area.

IDEA #8:
Become the
Real Estate Mayor
of Your Target Areas

It is important that you get involved in your local community as much as possible. City Council meetings, HOA meetings, PTA, church, local committees and neighborhood watch are all examples of ways you can get involved and serve the local area. Remember, you are running for the office of *"Real Estate Major"* of your farm!

Once you pick your area, you will build your business there through consistent marketing, exposure, branding, involvement and advertising.

Imagine that you were running for mayor of your city. What would that look like?

What kind of marketing campaigns would you employ in order to get the vote?

Visualize your mayoral campaign.

Well, farming looks the same way; only you are running for mayor of a smaller territory – more like a precinct, subdivision or an area of town.

Your Territory Should Be Nearby

Dominating an area that is near where you work or live helps put the fun and excitement into becoming the RE Mayor in that area. You can pop by your client's house at a moment's notice. Plus you get the added benefit of getting to see your marketing efforts at work on a constant basis, as you drive through these nearby areas.

If you choose an area that is too far away from where you live, you will find yourself regretting making that long drive. I recommend that you keep this area within 5 to 10 minutes of where you live, if at all possible.

Of course you can take listings in a very large area, if it's part of your MLS and if you are familiar with the area, but I do not recommend becoming the RE Mayor in those faraway areas, unless I can partner with a nearby agent.

Personally, I used to take listings in five counties. I don't mind driving an hour to a listing appointment, but I don't try to dominate this area. The area you *campaign and reign* should be close to your home base.

"What if the Area I Want is Already Dominated by a Competitor?"

I suggest you begin with an area that doesn't appear to be heavily farmed or heavily dominated currently. Drive around and check out the signs that are out. You can also run MLS reports to see who dominates the listings in that area.

If you feel that you absolutely must break into a particular area, go ahead and begin farming there. If that area is already heavily farmed by another agent, just realize that it can take longer to make headway. It can be done, but the fruits of your labor may come further down the road.

Chapter Homework

Watch Knolly's FREE Videos for this Chapter to help you grow your success even faster! To watch simply go to
Knolly.com/FreeTMLVideos
or scan the QR Code Below of the video you want to watch.

Videos Included for this Chapter:

☐ **How to Become the Real Estate Mayor of YOUR AREA (Real Estate Lead Gen Secrets Part 7 Of 12)**

☐ HOW TO BECOME THE REAL ESTATE MAYOR OF YOUR AREA

IDEA #9:
Create an Area Facebook Community (Group) and YouTube Channel

You can easily start a Facebook Community (a Facebook Group) for the various neighborhoods and area that you serve, and provide invaluable content to your community members.

Do video interviews with local business owners and local restaurants and feature them and their businesses on your channel. You can also talk about new businesses and municipal services that are coming into the area.

Here Are Some Of The Folks You Can Interview:

- Restaurant owners/managers;
- Local Banks and Credit Unions;
- Government officials;
- Hospital/emergency clinic directors;
- Large employers;
- Service providers.

Interview Examples:

- Interview a local landscaper in the spring with questions like: *"When is the best time to fertilize your lawn?"* and *"When is the best time to begin planting spring Annuals?"*
- Interview a local gym owner about the best exercises for folks who work in an office environment or just ask questions about their facility and what they have to offer the community.
- Interview a local health organization to find out what services are available to the local community.
- Interview a new restaurant or your favorite area boutique shops.

Your community Facebook page will absolutely help to submit you as the preferred agent in your target area. Make sure that you are consistently shooting videos and posting them in both your Facebook group and your YouTube channel.

Besides interviewing local business owners you can also post your open houses, new listings and recent sales, as well as area real estate sales statistics.

Chapter Homework

Watch Knolly's FREE Videos for this Chapter to help you grow your success even faster! To watch simply go to
Knolly.com/FreeTMLVideos
or scan the QR Code Below of the video you want to watch.

Videos Included for this Chapter:

☐ **Get MORE LISTINGS by Creating an Area Facebook Group and YouTube Channel**

☐ **Launching a Local Facebook Group and Youtube Channel (Real Estate Lead Gen Secrets Part 8 of 12)**

☐ **How NOT to Look Stupid On Video and Magnetize Your Ideal Clients in Your Business**

IDEA #10:
Host a "Neighborhood Event" as Your Open Houses

Instead of just hosting an open house, make sure that you were hosting an "event."

You could have wine tastings from the local winery, barbecue from a local barbecue joint or food tasting from a local restaurant.

Make this a community event, not just a plain old open house.

Hosting it as event will make all the neighbors want to list with YOU when the time comes to sell their home!

Whether you like doing open houses or not, the fact remains that open houses can serve a major purpose when your goal is to dominate your farm area through branding.

Having 20 to 30 signs on the street corners around your farm area every weekend is a strong way to create a credible and sustained presence in your farm.

Once you have a listing in your farm area, do as many open houses as you can and be sure to personally invite the neighbors to your open house event.

This is hard work but it is a proven method.

Some of the visitors to your open house will be future sellers and at your open house event they will get to see your stellar marketing in practice.

Chapter Homework

Watch Knolly's FREE Video for this Chapter to help you grow your
success even faster! To watch simply go to
Knolly.com/FreeTMLVideos
or scan the QR Code Below to watch.

Videos Included for this Chapter:

☐ **Host Neighborhood Events to BOOST Your
Listing Inventory**

IDEA #11:
Mail to Every Home in Your Farm Every Month

EDDM is an incredible gift introduced by the United States Postal Service. With EDDM, you can send a jumbo postcard to every home in your farm area for less than twenty cents each.

You don't even have to affix the postage stamps or address labels. You simply pick the area you want your postcards *delivered* to, fill out a form, and deliver the postcards to the Post Office.

To enjoy ultimate Success with Listings, I believe that you should strive to employ LOW or NO COST strategies. Farming does not have to be expensive; in fact it can be *free*. Say what!? Yes, it's true.

Using EDDM currently costs less 20¢ per house to send your mailing piece.

Farming for FREE

Now let's suppose your farm was 500 houses. Mailing to your farm would cost just under $100 in postage. All you need to do is invite four service providers to participate in your mailer. Each trade will receive a small ad on the back of your postcard and they each invest just $25. Now how much will it cost to you to mail your marketing piece? *Nothing.*

If you charged each one $40, you would cover the postage and the cost of printing your postcards as well.

Local trade vendors make good candidates. For forty bucks they can piggyback on your mailer and reach 500 houses. At just eight cents per house, that's a phenomenal deal. If your farm were 1000 houses you would charge $80 per trade, and so on. You can also include more than 4 trades and bring the price down further for each participant.

"Who are the Best Trades to Partner With?"

Below is an alphabetical list of some of the best local trades you can consider partnering with.

- ☐ Air Conditioning;
- ☐ Appliance Repair;
- ☐ Attorneys;
- ☐ Auto Repairing & Service;
- ☐ Burglar Alarm Systems;
- ☐ Carpet and Rug Cleaners;
- ☐ Cleaning Services;
- ☐ Computer Service & Repair;
- ☐ Concrete Contractors;

☐ Contractors – General;

☐ Deck Builders;

☐ Doors – Garage Doors;

☐ Dry Wall Contractors;

☐ Electrical;

☐ Fence;

☐ Flooring;

☐ Florists;

☐ Foundation Repair;

☐ Furniture Dealers;

☐ Handyman Service;

☐ Home Inspection;

☐ Home Remodeling;

☐ Home Warranty;

☐ Insurance Agent;

☐ Lawn Maintenance/Landscaping;

☐ Locksmith;

☐ Mason Contractors;

☐ Mortgage Lender;

☐ Moving Services;

☐ Painters;

☐ Pest Control;

☐ Plumbing Services;

☐ Roofing Companies;

☐ Septic Installation;

☐ Siding Contractors;

☐ Storage – Household & Commercial;

☐ Title Companies;

☐ Tree Service;

☐ Windows.

IDEA #12:
Create Your
Pre-Listing Video
(Your Virtual Listing
Presentation)

You should think of the Virtual Listing Presentation or pre-listing video as your *"promo reel"*. Every famous person has one, and YOU should too!

This virtual listing presentation is a 3 to 10 minute video that highlights you and your team. This video will serve as a condensed and highly concentrated version of your listing presentation, designed to win the trust and confidence of your prospective seller before they meet with you.

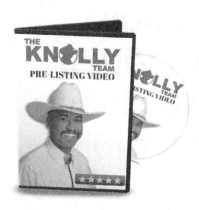

In this video you will emphasize your marketing plan, how your team operates, pricing the house, how commission works and why the prospective seller should trust you with the sale of their house.

It is amazing to see the impact that your pre-listing video has on your prospects when it is coupled with your seller book and your pre-listing package.

A few weeks ago I was at a listing appointment and the seller would not stop smiling the entire time we were together.

Because the seller had already viewed my pre-listing presentation, read my book and reviewed the pre-listing package, there wasn't really much to discuss except price. We sat there reviewing the price while the seller kept smiling at me and saying *"Yes, Knolly – whatever you think is best is OK with me. I'm trusting your judgment on that."*

Once your sellers read your book and watch your "movie" they will feel like they already know you and trust you. In fact, when you effectively integrate these tools into your listing business, you can cut half of the time off your listing appointment.

⟹ TIMESAVER

In my **"Overnight Celebrity" Done-For-You Toolkit** you get a copy of my video along with a complete editable script for FREE! The complete Toolkit is available at NO COST TO YOU.

Find out more at: SuccessWithListings.com/more-info

IDEA #13:
Create Your
Pre-Listing Package
(Your Press Kit)

In addition to your seller book, a complete pre-listing package is essential to your success in the listings game because in today's competitive environment, you want to win the listing before you show up to the listing appointment.

In other words, you want to influence your seller prospects to decide to list with you, before they ever sit down with you.

Think of your pre-listing package as your press kit. All famous people have one. Just imagine you were going after an important role in a movie. You would likely have to submit your press kit before being called in for an audition.

Sure, if you are Denzel Washington or Julia Roberts you could probably skip this step, but if you are any of the other 29 actors in the film you had better send your press kit in advance!

In your successful listing business your press kit serves the important role of convincing the decision makers to consider auditioning you for the job of selling their house.

Likewise, if you were going for an important job at any company, they would want to see your resume and qualifications before considering you as a candidate for the position.

No one shows up at a job interview or a movie audition without first sending over their credentials. Yet I am still amazed at the many agents who will seek to have a prospect trust them with their *life-savings* without sending over their complete pre-listing package beforehand. Not doing this puts you at a disadvantage.

Perhaps you are already great at getting people to trust you. Perhaps you don't currently use a pre-listing package and don't see the need for one since you typically are able to walk away from the interview with the listing secured.

Even so, if you don't have a pre-listing packet you are using a system that is outdated, less productive and inefficient. If you are good without a pre-listing packet, you will be on fire *with* one.

Along with your book (Idea #14), your pre-listing package will "toot your horn" for you so that you can spend far less time at each listing appointment. In fact, by the time you sit down with your prospect they should already be sold on you.

You want to make sure that your seller prospects receive a copy of our pre-listing package before you show up for the listing appointment. You, your Admin, a team member or a runner will hand-deliver it a day or two beforehand.

Here are several key ingredients to a winning pre-listing package:

- ☐ Cover Page.
- ☐ Cover Letter.
- ☐ Marketing Plan.
- ☐ Testimonials (Reviews/Results/Case Studies).
- ☐ Special Report: Top 4 Reasons Homes Don't Sell.
- ☐ Agent Interview Sheet.
- ☐ Top 10 Reasons to List With Me.
- ☐ Seller Homework: Why My Home is Special.
- ☐ Seller Homework: My Upgrades.
- ☐ Seller Homework: Property Information Sheet.
- ☐ Home Prep Tips.
- ☐ Top Tips on Showing Your Home.

☐ Cover Page

Colorful and impressive, the cover page is used to "wow" the client from the onset. You can have the cover page printed on thick stock - almost like a book cover.

☐ Cover Letter

The cover letter introduces you and briefly explains how you will meet their needs. It also serves as a table of contents.

☐ Marketing Plan

Your marketing plan is essential. Your one page marketing plan shows an easy-to-follow plan for getting their house sold. It sets you apart from other agents, because most don't have a written marketing plan. The marketing plan is written in a bulleted format and covers your strategy in the following areas:

1. Outdoor Advertising
2. Internet Advertising
3. Print Advertising
4. Premium Marketing
5. Industry Marketing

☐ Testimonials (Reviews/Results/Case Studies)

Your pre-listing package should include a page with 7 or more testimonials. Getting testimonials is an absolute must – even if you are new to the business. I've usually found it more effective to write the testimonials on behalf of my client. I simply call them and ask them how they would describe working with me. I let them speak and I take notes. I then email them a 2-3 sentence testimonial written based on our conversation and ask them if it correctly articulates what they said. This can be a time saver, because oftentimes folks with good intentions just don't get around to writing out their own testimonial.

For new agents, my suggestion is to get some testimonials that are generic and written to show sellers that you are trustworthy. If you don't have a lot of past clients, you can get some testimonials from your previous career. Here's an example of a testimonial from a previous co-worker: *"Ray is great to work with and has always been a team player. He is very honest and always put my interests above his own."* You can see how this type of testimonial can really come from anyone – and isn't specific to selling houses. Get at least 7 of these for your testimonials section.

☐ Special Report: Top 4 Reasons Homes Don't Sell.

Some years ago I put together a special report entitled *Top 4 Reasons Homes Don't Sell*. At the time I was working with lots and lots of Expired listings, and after listing hundreds of them I began to notice a pattern as to why these properties failed to sell.

Obviously the top reason was price, but there were more subtle reasons like having bad photos or having an agent that other agents in town don't want to work with. Sometimes an inexperienced agent will not know how to hold a deal together, so a listing could fall out of contract and fail to sell. This document helps sellers see that you understand why homes don't sell and assures them that you will avoid those pitfalls.

☐ Agent Interview Sheet.

Your Agent Interview Sheet is an ingenious document designed to completely crush your competition. It dispels the common consumer view that all agents are created equal and gives your clients the confidence to trust you with their most valuable asset. It also reinforces that they are making the right decision in hiring you. This sheet is particularly useful when a seller is considering interviewing more than one agent.

I recently talked with a seller who was looking to interview 14 agents! Yikes! Her property had failed to sell with her previous agent, so she wasn't going to make the mistake of hiring the wrong agent this time around. With this one sheet alone she was able to narrow her list down to just two agents that she wanted to interview – me and one other. 24 hours later she called to inform me that they were listing with me. This one document helped her eliminate 12 competitors.

Most sellers won't want to interview 14 agents. In fact, according to a recent NAR survey, nearly 70% of sellers interview just ONE agent prior to listing their house, so much of what I will teach you in this book will be geared toward getting you to be the one that gets in front of them first!

On the other hand, about 30% of sellers will want to interview more than one agent. This interview sheet will help you gain the advantage over your competitors.

I always want to know if a seller prospect is considering interviewing more than one agent. If they are, I will make sure that they use my interview sheet to conduct these interviews.

Here is the script that we use:

You: Cathy – are you going to be interviewing more than one agent for the job of selling your house?

Prospect: Well yes actually, I'm thinking about interviewing three.

You: That's great Cathy. Let me ask you – what specific criteria are you using to decide which agents you will allow into your house for a sit down interview?

Prospect: Uhhh – Well... I want to make sure they are good and I have to feel comfortable with them.

You: "That's great, Cathy! You know I've found that there are 10 specific questions you should ask any agent before you agree to list your house. Since I work with real estate agents every day, I know which questions you absolutely need to ask. In fact – I recommend that you ask these questions over the phone before you agree to meet with them. Think of this as a job interview process. You don't want to waste your time sitting down with anyone who doesn't meet the qualifications for the job. By the way Cathy – I've typed up those 10 questions and I can send you a copy. Would that be helpful to you?"

Prospect: Absolutely.

You: Wonderful, Cathy. I'll go ahead and email it over to you. It's a handy one page PDF with the top 10 questions and it already contains my answers to those questions. There's also space to write down the other agent's answer. You'll simply let the other agent know that you have a few questions to ask – and that you will get back with them if you would like to meet in person. It's a pretty simple process.

Prospect: Great! Thank You!

The beauty of the agent interview sheet is that you get to decide the questions you use! You should also include a portion where the seller can add up the score (how many questions were answered correctly).

You can come up with whatever questions you feel are appropriate, and you don't have to use 10.

Whenever you provide this information to a potential seller, they will feel indebted to you for providing them with a system they can use which makes their life easier. You also have a convenient excuse to call the seller back and gain their confidence. This form is definitely a game changer.

☐ Top 10 Reasons to Trust Me with the Sale of Your House!

People love Top 10 lists. Since securing the listing begins with securing the trust of the prospect, you want to give your prospects reasons why they should trust you with the sale of their most valuable asset.

Your Top 10 list also reinforces to the prospect that they are making the right decision by hiring you.

Think of 10 reasons why someone should trust you with the sale of their house.

Write down these 10 reasons and then expound on each one with a sentence or two.

☐ Seller Homework (Page 1): Why My Home is Special

My good friend and mentor Rand Smith taught me the importance of having Seller Homework in my pre-listing packet. It has been an invaluable addition!

This sheet helps you get the full scoop on the property so that you can write a glowing property description.

On this fill-in-the blank sheet, your seller will list the features they really enjoyed most about their house, the type of person they think would love it, how they would best describe their house to a potential buyer and what features they liked most about the neighborhood/area.

Another trick is that whenever I write the *property description* for the listing, I use many of the adjectives and pick up on the features and benefits that the seller keyed in on. They love it!

When they read my property description they always feel like I nailed it, and they often will say "Knolly, you described it perfectly!"

Filling out this sheet also helps your seller prepare to sell and to emotionally detach from the property.

Here is the information we request on this special form:

- Home features that we have really enjoyed: _____.

- The type of person I think would love this home most is: _____.

- …because of these features: _____.

- How would you describe your home to a buyer?

  _____

- What are the features you like most about your neighborhood/area: _____?

☐ Seller Homework (Page 2): My Property Upgrades.

Knowing the specific upgrades that your client did to the property helps you to get your client top dollar. This sheet gives you negotiating leverage over the competition and also helps you write great ad copy for the listing.

This sheet allows the seller to list all of the upgrades that they made to the property including the interior, exterior, landscaping, and additional buildings.

Your seller will list the approximate amount they spent on each upgrade (or the approximate value of the upgrade if they did it themselves). Once you total up all the upgrades, you can use this total as negotiating leverage.

☐ Seller Homework: Property Information Sheet (Pages 3 and 4)

For my team, I designed a 2 page form which we call the Property Information Sheet. This sheet serves as a checklist of the most important property features and allows you, your seller or a team member to quickly check off the key features of the house.

Although your MLS may also have such a document, it will generally be too exhaustive. Your sheet should focus on the listing features that are most important to potential buyers (based on the most popular online search criteria).

A few years after developing this document, I began experimenting with asking my sellers to fill it out. As a result, we now save at least 20 minutes on each listing appointment and the information is more accurate. Now we simply make this document part of the seller homework.

Here's the script to effectively use when requesting that the seller fill out this information:

You: You know Steve, we used to fill out this information ourselves, but you know what we found?

Seller: What's that?

You: In order to get you top dollar for your house, we found that it is best for the homeowner to fill out this form. We don't want to miss anything. Since you've lived in the house for more than nine years and I've only been at your house for a little over an hour - you are far more qualified to put down the most accurate information. Does that make sense?

Seller: You bet it does! I'll get it filled out right away.

You: Awesome Steve! It shouldn't take you more than 20 minutes, and you can email it to me!

☐ Top Tips on Preparing Your Home for Sale

This is a two-page checklist that you can use to guide your seller on the top things they can do to prepare their house for sale.

This checklist allows the seller to walk through the house on their own and identify the things they should do to prepare their property for a successful sale and to get top dollar.

These tips give the seller no future excuse when negative showing feedback is received. It also allows you to sell their house faster and for more money.

☐ Top Tips on Showing Your Home.

This one page document gives your seller a checklist of best practices when it comes to showing the house. It also gives them no future excuse when negative feedback is received as a result of their house not being show-ready.

You will want to encourage your sellers to give a copy of this checklist to everyone who is living in the house (and to tenants) so that they can also get in on the act.

Don't expect your sellers to simply remember the things that you've told them regarding preparing their house for sale and handling showings. Using written checklists (that you can point the seller back to) is a much better system.

⟹ TIMESAVER

In my **"Overnight Celebrity" Done-For-You Toolkit** you get my complete and editable Pre-Listing Package for FREE! The Toolkit is available at NO COST TO YOU.

Find out more at: SuccessWithListings.com/more-info

Chapter Homework

Watch Knolly's FREE Videos for this Chapter to help you grow your success even faster! To watch simply go to
Knolly.com/FreeTMLVideos
or scan the QR Code Below of the video you want to watch.

Videos Included for this Chapter:

☐ **Creating Your Pre-Listing Package (Your Press Kit) - Lead Gen Secrets Part 9 of 12**

☐ **The 3 Secret Tools of a Top Listing Agent**

☐ GET MORE LISTINGS NOW by Creating Your Pre-Listing Package (Your Press Kit)

IDEA #14:
Write Your Seller BOOK (or License Knolly's for FREE)

For thousands of years mankind has used tools to make life on planet earth successful and easier. As you venture into any new enterprise, you will need both skills and tools.

Now suppose you were a professional flooring installer and you had all the skills and qualifications, but you didn't have the right tools.

Will you get the job?

Probably not.

All the skill in the world won't help you if you don't have the tools necessary to get the job done right.

If you have all the tools to lay carpet, yet the majority of your prospects want tile or wood flooring, you won't event get a chance to bid on the job.

No matter how good you are at laying tile, you won't get the job if you don't have the tools.

Too many agents are showing up at the listing appointment with the wrong tools, or no tools at all.

It's no wonder they are generating less than optimal success. If you are switching from a buyer focused business to focusing on more listings, you will need the right tools.

Here are the tools of a celebrity:

1. Your Book (this is your complete seller's guide).

2. Your Press Kit (this is your complete pre-listing package) (Idea #13).

3. Your Movie (this is your virtual listing presentation) (Idea #12).

In your listing business, you should implement these 3 essential tools: your book (most celebrities have one), your press kit (pre-listing package), and your movie (high quality pre-listing video). Of course you will supplement these 3 core tools with several of the other 27 Ideas.

YOUR SELLER BOOK (YOUR COMPLETE GUIDE FOR SELLERS)

It is very common for a well-known person to have a book. Whenever I pass out my book to prospects, their reaction is the same "Wow! You have a book?!" I cannot tell you how many houses I have listed as a result of my Seller's Book alone!

Besides making an impression, your well-written book allows you to connect with sellers and leverage your time.

What if you actually had the time to divulge all of your wisdom and knowledge to a seller, and give them the full benefit of your acumen? What would you say? This is where your book comes in.

Your book greatly leverages your time because it allows you to sit down with a potential seller and share with them the entire selling process from A-Z, without being physically present.

In addition to allowing you to immediately be viewed as a top expert in your area, your book also greatly leverages your time.

Your book allows you to eliminate four to seven or more hours of your time over the life of each listing. So if you plan to list 50 houses this year, your book should save you about 200 to 350 hours! How much is your time worth?

How to Write Your Book

You can write your seller book in just eight chapters. Your book should be filled with useful information along with photos and illustrations as necessary.

Your Seller Book Chapter 1 – *Deciding to Sell.*

Oftentimes the folks that you give a copy of your book to are just *thinking about selling.* The first chapter should be written to help them through the decision-making process. This chapter helps them to prepare mentally and emotionally for selling. It also aids them in examining their motives and reasons for selling – so that they make the best decision for themselves and their family.

We've all had would-be sellers who don't want to meet with us right away because they haven't made their mind up yet and they don't want us to "try to sell them". They don't want to feel pressured, or perhaps they just don't want to waste your valuable time. Now your answer to this put-off is quite simple:

You: You know Kelly – I can appreciate that you are just considering the idea of selling and aren't really sure at this time. Here's a copy of my book that I wrote to help my clients through the entire process.

Prospect: Wow! Well, thanks!

This approach will gain you more trust and win you more listings because you will be viewed as a dynamic (low pressure) consultant with their best interests at heart. Plus, you now have a great excuse to make periodic follow up calls to the prospect.

Your Seller Book Chapter 2 – *Marketing Your House for Sale*

You will use this chapter to outline your complete marketing plan. If you've done any number of listings, you know that sellers always want to know *"what are you going to do to market my house?"* This chapter outlines your complete plan for the successful sale of their property.

Your Seller Book Chapter 3 – *Pricing Your House.*

This chapter is written to show sellers everything that is involved in arriving at the correct price of their house. Everything from how price is determined, how to interpret a

CMA, how the buyer's appraisal will affect price, and how pricing affects showings should be discussed here. This chapter saves you the time of having to explain these concepts at the listing appointment.

Your Seller Book Chapter 4 – *Getting Your House Ready for the Market.*

Getting their property ready for the market allows your clients to enjoy receiving the highest price possible for their property. This chapter explains the top 3 things they can do (declutter, clean and paint) and why these things are so important. This chapter should discuss staging as well, and you will want to include a complete checklist of things they can do to the exterior, interior, kitchen, bath and much more. This chapter should also contain a list of minor repairs that are typically recommended.

This chapter saves you tons of time because it allows the seller to walk through their own house at their leisure and make their own checklist of items that need to be addressed prior to you putting their house on the market.

Your Seller Book Chapter 5 – *Choosing the Right Agent.*

This chapter is dedicated to explaining to your prospects why YOU are the best agent for the job of getting their house sold. It is unfortunate that many sellers still believe that all agents are the same. This chapter serves to dispel that myth and makes the case for why they should hire YOU!

Your Seller Book Chapter 6 – *Handling Showings.*

This chapter of your book also leverages your time because it explains to your seller in detail how showings should be conducted. This chapter also consults your clients on how they should conduct showings of the property if it is rented (has tenants) and gives them a handy showing checklist.

Your Seller Book Chapter 7 – *Working with Offers.*

This chapter serves to enlighten your clients on how to review an offer. This chapter points out the most important paragraphs in the contract and gives your clients your best advice on how to interpret the information. Whenever you receive an offer on a client's house, you will simply call and use the following script:

You: Hi Samantha! Good News! We received an offer on your house!

Prospect: Great!

You: Now, Samantha - I'm going to email you the offer right now. I want you to go back and read chapter 7 of my book along with the offer and then let's discuss any questions you have.

Prospect: Sounds good!

Before using my book, I spent countless hours explaining to my sellers how financing works, earnest money, buyer closing costs, settlement expenses, the buyer's inspection process and on and on. I have completely eliminated these conversations with this one chapter.

Your Seller Book Chapter 8 – *Closing On the Sale.*

This chapter helps your clients understand everything that is involved with successfully closing their transaction. Here you will also discuss the buyer inspection process.

You are preparing the seller by explaining how the process works so they won't have any surprises. The chapter also discusses what they need to bring to closing, how to prepare for the day of closing and should provide a handy moving checklist.

How Your Seller Book Leverages Your Time.

Your book not only makes you look like the rock star that you are, it also serves to shave at least 3 hours of your time off the life of every listing you take, and helps you generate more seller leads.

Your book will shave at least 30 minutes off your listing presentation time alone because the sellers you meet with are already educated on the process and what you can do for them.

Your book can shave many weeks off the listing time on market, because it educates your sellers about pricing so that you can get it priced right at the beginning of the listing term.

Your book helps convince your seller prospects that they absolutely should *list with you.*

Your book helps your sellers make the right first impression and generate more offers by teaching them how to prepare their house for sale.

Your book helps you save at least an hour during the offer negotiation stage because it helps your seller better understand the process and sets their expectation up front. Your book also helps to generate you more listing referrals.

Most of the real estate agents I train don't have a seller's book. Of the few that do, most of them have one that that is stapled, spiral bound or in a three-hole punched notebook. While there is nothing inherently wrong with that approach, it does not convey the look of a celebrity.

The seller book I wrote and use doesn't look like something that was created at a local copy shop or printed on a fancy laser printer. It's a real book.

Your seller book should look and feel as professional as any book that your seller currently has on their bookshelf. You can have your book printed at a number of places for a cost of less than $3 each so it's not expensive at all.

Plus, with book printers that offer *printing on demand,* you can print as few as 25 copies at a time. There is absolutely no excuse for you not to look your best.

A 24/7 Virtual Assistant

Imagine hiring a virtual assistant to be your promoter, doing nothing but going out and helping you generate listings. That's what you book and pre-listing package do. They work for you while you are sleeping!

Now imagine paying this person a one-time fee and having them work for you for the rest of your career!

That's what you get when you snap my complete toolkit into your listing business.

Getting Your Complete Seller Book and Tools for *FREE*

To allow us to be able to license it to others at no charge, we incorporated a *Preferred Vendor Directory* right onto the back cover, so that the complete cost is paid for by your preferred vendors.

You can license my book and get your books printed at no cost to you! It's rather simple. Your customizable book comes with an editable back cover.

On the back cover there are 6 ad slots for service trades and one banner position for a preferred vendor. You will earn at least $900 each and every year that you are using this tool! This means your sponsors cover the entire cost of licensing your book plus you can print more than 300 copies a year at no cost to you.

I give you a complete system for generating your book sponsors including call and email scripts and a back cover template that you can snap in.

Tools Included in My Complete System:

The tools including in my system are:

- ✓ Your Complete Seller Book (editable)
- ✓ Easy to Edit Book Cover
- ✓ Complete Vendor System to cover the entire cost and generate annual revenues to you (comes with vendor email and call scripts and vendor payment form)
- ✓ BONUS 1: My Editable Pre-Listing Package
- ✓ BONUS 2: My Virtual Listing Presentation (Pre-Listing Video) with editable video script
- ✓ BONUS 3: Job Descriptions for 14 Team Members (editable)
- ✓ BONUS 4: Listing Team Training Manual (editable)

Your Complete Seller Book
This is my editable book with copyright license. No need to pay a ghostwriter.

Your Editable Pre-Listing Package
Editable version of the pre-listing we use every day to list and sell properties. 14 pages of documents that you can edit and use in your business.

Your Virtual Listing Presentation (Pre-Listing Video)

You get a copy of the pre-listing video that my team uses to educate sellers along with an editable script so you can easily create your own video.

Job Descriptions for 14 Team Members

Comprehensive list of editable job descriptions for 14 different team positions.

Administrative Assistant | Buyer Specialist | CEO
Executive Assistant | Marketing Assistant | Office Manager
Listing Manager Showing Assistant| Team Runner
Short Sale Processor | Short Sale Listing Manager | Team Agent
Telemarketer | Transaction Coordinator

Your Listing Team Training Manual

24 pages and completely editable, this is the same manual I use to train my listing team members.

For more information or to get yours go to: bit.ly/tmltoolkit.

Final Thoughts

Whether you decide to use the tools I have created or develop your own is up to you.

Either way I admonish you to begin implementing these important tools in your business immediately so that you can reap the rewards of more listings, more income for your family and more time to enjoy life.

➡️ TIMESAVER

In my **"Overnight Celebrity" Done-For-You Toolkit** you get a copy of my Editable Book (Your Seller Guide) along with a complete editable script for FREE! The complete Toolkit is available at NO COST TO YOU.

Find out more at: SuccessWithListings.com/more-info

Chapter Homework

Watch Knolly's FREE Videos for this Chapter to help you grow your success even faster! To watch simply go to
Knolly.com/FreeTMLVideos
or scan the QR Code Below of the video you want to watch.

Videos Included for this Chapter:

☐ **Your Editable Real Estate Seller Guide (Customizable Seller Book)- Lead Gen Secrets Part 10 of 12**

☐ **How to Get MORE LISTINGS! (with your FREE Customizable Seller Guide!)**

☐ **LISTING SCRIPTS! Knolly shares some of his best Success with Listings Scripts!**

IDEA #15:
Circle Prospecting Strategy Around Your Just Listeds

Circle Prospecting is the process of knocking on 100 doors around the "subject property." You can even circle prospect around a property you've sold in the past, or one that your office sold or currently has listed.

The door knocking script around circle prospecting is real simple. The best way to build rapport with a stranger is to get them to talk about their favorite subject: themselves.

With this script, you will do just that. You will get prospects engaged and then you will earn the right to ask for their business.

JUST LISTED Door Knock:

You: Hi, Mr. & Mrs. Neighbor, my name is _____ with _____ Realty. I'm hoping you can help me! I just listed your neighbor's house at 123 Main St and I was hoping you could share with me 2 or 3 reasons why you love living here?

You: .....oh awesome! That will really help me in delivering you a new neighbor! By the way, now is your time to have a hand in selecting your new neighbor. Who do you know in your network that's thinking about making a move? I know this is a tough neighborhood to get into and inventory is really scarce....

....thank you so much for putting me in touch with those people....

[If no names come to mind ask the neighbor to call you directly when they do, better yet ask them for their contact info so you can follow up]

You: Lastly, because this house is going to move so quickly, my next challenge will be how to help all of our clients find the next house that will be coming available in the neighborhood. We already are talking to dozens of potential buyers. That's what makes us different than other REALTORS®, we actually prospect for buyers for our sellers! So, do you know anyone that's also thinking about making a move?

Circle prospect around other agent's listings.

On any "Just Listeds" in your farm, why not also circle prospect around that listing? Even though it is not yours, you can tell homeowners that you noticed a house just came up for sale in "your market area" and move forward with a modification of the circle prospecting script above.

This means you could be out circle prospecting any time there is a new listing in your target area!

IDEA #16:
Circle Prospecting
Strategy Around Your
Contract Pendings

Once you have the property under contract, go back to the 100 homes around the subject property using the following script:

You: Well actually that great house at 123 Main went under contract in only 4 days.... Here's my stack of offers of other buyers who wanted to buy in the neighborhood but got outbid.... It's evident that prices are on the rise. Do you know of anyone since our last chat that's thinking about making a move?

If you received multiple offers, let them know! For example you could show up at the door with two or three offers in your hand! That communicates and relays urgency and let them know that you need more inventory because you already know who the buyers are!

IDEA #17:
Circle Prospecting Strategy Around Your Just Solds

Now then, once the house closes escrow you go back to let the neighbors know!

 You: Hi Mr. and Mrs. Neighbor, we wanted to hand off the latest sales report in the neighborhood and let you know that Mr. and Mrs. New Neighbor just moved in down the street and they are awesome people so please welcome them to the block when you get a chance. I'd love to send you my monthly newsletter so would it be ok to get a personal email address so we can keep you better informed with the trends of the local market?

Be sure to take a flyer or postcard showing your listing that sold and what the recent sales in the area are. Having a JUST SOLD gives you the perfect excuse to canvas the neighborhood!!

Remember, you can use this strategy with your office as well!

For example if anyone else in your office sold a house in the area, you can just change the script and say "our office recently sold 101 Hickory Cove".

IDEA #18:
Become a Trusted
Resource for FSBOs

For a variety of reasons, some sellers choose to try and sell their home themselves and for most this proves to be a losing proposition.

The statistical facts prove that homeowners will net a LOT less money, and take a lot longer to sell when trying to sell their home themselves instead of hiring you to get it SOLD.

According to NAR's For Sale By Owner (FSBO) Statistics, 9% of U.S. homes sold FSBO.

Knowing what goes into a top dollar sale, it's not surprising that the data reveals the typical FSBO home sold for 18.65% less than similar properties that were properly marketed and exposed by a licensed REALTOR®.

Let's examine why this is the case.

When a person decides to represent themselves in a court of law, the opposing attorney will immediately see an "opportunity".

In the same way, prospective buyers will see an opportunity with someone trying to sell their own home.

The #1 reason some sellers try to sell on their own is to get out of paying the agent commission.

Because a great listing agent can statistically net 8-9% more for their clients, the FSBO would actually loose a great deal of money (and time) trying to sell themselves.

In most cases, the FSBO will agree to pay a 3% (or so) commission to the buyer agent who finds a buyer for the home. This means the 'perceived' savings is now 3%.

However, when you take into account the fact that homes properly marketed generate an 8 to 19% higher sales price, it becomes apparent that most FSBOs can actually net 5 to 16% less than hiring than they would by hiring a REALTOR® to do everything for them!

Knolly's FSBO Pop-By Script:

Script! "Hi there!

"My name is ___ with _____"

"I noticed that your house is on the market for sale and we have a lot of buyers who are looking in the area. When is the best time to bring my potential buyers by to take a look at your house? Do you prefer afternoons or are evenings better?

"GREAT!"

"By the way - when would be the best time for me to preview your house before I begin bringing my prospective buyers over?"

The idea with a FSBO is that you want to build rapport with them.

As you preview their home, make sure you give them a copy of your book which will engage them and help strike up a dialogue.

You can say things like: "You know John, I know that you are set on selling your house yourself. Still, I would be happy to answer any real estate related questions you need help with. My advice is always free"

Keep checking in with seller periodically to see how the sale is going (and see what question you can answer from your book) and offer any advice you can (within reason).

Quick FSBO Facts to keep in mind:

1. Most FSBOs have a good SOI that you can tap into. Most of their friends and family will NOT try what they are attempting, so even if they don't list with you they can easily refer their family and friends to you.

2. The FSBO may also need to BUY and you can pick them up on the buy side if you build a good rapport with them.

3. Most FSBOs are just "testing the waters" but will hire an agent once they are fed up with the process or when the process becomes too time-consuming or daunting. You want to be first in line!

Let FSBOs know that you are available to host an open house event (Idea #10) for their property!

This helps get you in front of the neighbors and shows what you can do to the FSBO.

Before you agree to host an open house for them check with your brokerage for specific policies and how to go about this.

When hosting an open house for a FSBO (and when working with other potential sellers who are 'on the fence' about listing) you might consider offering a "trial listing" for say 7-10 days.

Of course the listing can always be extended if you don't get a good offer and the seller sees that you are doing a great job!

Ask the FSBOs you begin working with who they know that is looking to buy or sell. Since 91% of sellers don't try FSBO – your FSBO connections should be able to send you multiple leads while they have their house for sale.

Chapter Homework

Watch Knolly's FREE Video for this Chapter to help you grow your
success even faster! To watch simply go to
Knolly.com/FreeTMLVideos
or scan the QR Code Below to watch.

Videos Included for this Chapter:

☐ **Real Estate Circle Prospecting and Working
with FSBOs (Real Estate Lead Gen Secrets Part
11 of 12)**

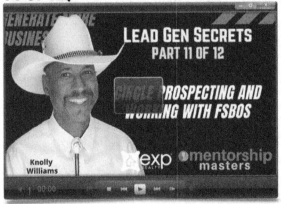

IDEA #19:
Become the Agent of Choice for Expireds

Expired Listings are Homes that were previously active on the MLS and failed to sell.

In the industry we call them Expireds.

When I first got into real estate in 2003, this was my number one strategy, especially since I was starting off in a new market where I had almost no SOI.

With Expireds, you can either call them or mail to them, or do a combination of both.

Most of the time sellers whose home failed to sell will be somewhat hostile toward real estate agents, because of their perceived bad experience with their previous agent. Just bear that in mind when you are calling them.

Your job is to show them that not all real estate agents are created equal, and that you are different.

FOR EXPIREDS - HERE'S THE METHOD I HAVE USED VERY SUCCESSFULLY AND SUGGEST:

First contact the expired seller using a script you like and discuss their situation over the phone.

If it appears that they will be listing their home again at some point in the future – and it looks like a listing you want to take on – ask them for their permission to send them a copy of your new book where you share with them your unique approach to getting their home sold.

Let them know that the book will be a valuable resource to them whether they list with you or not.

Then drop off the book (Idea #14) at their house along with your pre-listing package (Idea #13).

This will help you secure the listing when it comes time for them to list!

Keep in mind that, while going after Expireds is a good idea, it will likely result in a limited number of listings compared to the overall mix. But the more the merrier!

Expireds is a Niche strategy (and a good one) but keep in mind that as much as 70% of your business will come from your SOI, with 30% coming from both your Farm and your Niche.

Expireds is part of your Niche strategy.

Here's the Expired Script my team has used effectively for years (feel free to tweak it and use it!):

 Script to use when calling folks who are now Off the Market

Hi there Jim, my name is Barbara Riordan with the Knolly Team at eXp Realty.

Since your home recently went off the market, can we still let potential buyers know about it?
Y   N

Are you going to be interviewing real estate agents for the job of getting your home sold?
Y   N

_____

_____

_____

_____

3. Thanks Jim! Would you be offended if we drop off a free copy of Knolly's new book it's a complete guide to selling your home and we make it available to sellers for FREE in our market area. It's yours to keep whether you list with us or not, and it will really help you identify some of the things that may have gone wrong with your home sale.

If they ask *what is the book?* Let them know:

The book contains everything they need to know to either sell your home yourself, hire the right agent for the job of getting you home sold - or you may decide that right now may not be the best time for you to sell]

Q. Address to drop off to: _____

Q. What's your email address? _____

4. GREAT Jim! I'll have our Listing Manager Martin Jones call you so he can arrange to drop off a copy of Knolly's book!

Script to use if no answer: Hi there, my name is Barbara Johnson with the Knolly Team at eXp Realty.

Knolly has been ranked by Austin Business Journal by one of the top producing 7 agents in Austin and he wanted to see if we can be of help to you. Please call me at 512-206-0060 or email listings@knolly.com.

Also check out our website when you get a moment: www.Knolly.com.

We also want to drop off your free copy of Knolly's new book – it's a complete guide to selling your home. Again the number is 512-206-0060. Thanks!

Chapter Homework

Watch Knolly's FREE Videos for this Chapter to help you grow your success even faster! To watch simply go to
Knolly.com/FreeTMLVideos
or scan the QR Code Below of the video you want to watch.

Videos Included for this Chapter:

☐ **OLD EXPIREDS - Top 5 Real Estate NICHES in a DOWN MARKET (PART 2 of 7)**

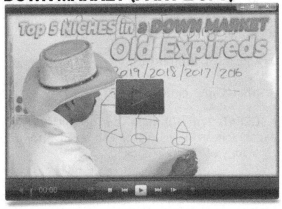

- **Niches = Riches: HOTTEST NICHES for MORE LISTING LEADS during a SHIFTING MARKET (w/Landvoice)**

IDEA #20:
Become the
Preferred Divorce
Sale Expert

Working the divorce niche can be very rewarding, but can also be very emotionally challenging if you do not know how to exercise detached compassion.

You cannot be emotionally attached to the outcome or the situation.

Couples facing divorce have a unique set of challenges when it comes to the sale of their home. Emotions can run high.

When faced with selling their home in the divorce process, the seller needs a REALTOR® who is trustworthy, compassionate, well-versed in the divorce home sale process and long on patience. The seller also needs to get the most money for their house in the least amount of time.

You have to understand and be OK with the fact that most couples facing divorce don't want to discuss the details regarding the home sale transaction jointly.

This means that selling a home in the divorce process can often require twice the amount of work for the real estate agent, because it is often necessary to communicate all of the details in separate and duplicate conversations.

You will also need to go to great lengths to ensure that all information shared with you is held in strictest confidence and confidentiality.

Achieving a successful divorce sale often begins with a private and confidential home sale consultation with each party individually.

You will also want to coordinate all of these details with each party's attorney and provide weekly status reports to all parties involved.

At the Knolly Team we have successfully worked with hundreds of sellers facing divorce and success can easily be achieved if you are willing to do the work.

To dominate in this niche you should partner with several divorce attorneys in your area and give them copies of your book (Idea #14) that they can hand out to their clients.

In fact, you should consider doing a unique version of your book and placing the divorce attorney on the entire back cover (for free).

Just change out the back cover - it's that simple!

You can create a version for each attorney you begin working with (the book will be the same inside and only the back cover will change).

Oftentimes in a court-ordered divorce sale, the judge will assign the real estate agent, and the attorney has a lot of pull when it comes to throwing your hat in the ring.

Be sure to create a flyer showcasing your Divorce Sale Services and begin circulating it to local family practice attorneys who specialize in divorce.

In addition, if you want to really cement the deal with an attorney you are trying to attract, be sure to interview them for your YouTube channel and Facebook Group (Idea #9)!

Chapter Homework

Watch Knolly's FREE Video for this Chapter to help you grow your success even faster! To watch simply go to
Knolly.com/FreeTMLVideos
or scan the QR Code below to watch.

Videos Included for this Chapter:

☐ **DIVORCE - Top 5 Real Estate NICHES in a DOWN MARKET (PART 5 of 7)**

IDEA #21:
Master the Luxury Market

Most agents aren't working the luxury market simply because they don't believe they belong there.

They lack confidence.

I implore you to make a solid decision to begin working the luxury niche, and then begin finding out all you can about the luxury market in your area.

I've sold hundreds of luxury homes and finally came to realize that high end sellers are just like everyone else.

They want you to do a great job for them and they are willing to pay you for your services. They are real people and most of them are pretty cool.

Besides, it doesn't typically take much more work and to sell a luxury home and it oftentimes requires less work, because the sellers are generally pretty business savvy and have sold properties before.

Learn as much as you can about the luxury market by taking courses, watching YouTube videos and attending training about the luxury marketplace in your local market.

Chapter Homework

Watch Knolly's FREE Video for this Chapter to help you grow your success even faster! To watch simply go to
Knolly.com/FreeTMLVideos
or scan the QR Code below to watch.

Videos Included for this Chapter:

☐ **Mastering the Luxury Market! (What Holds Most Agents Back)**

☐

IDEA #22:
Become the Trusted
Probate Expert

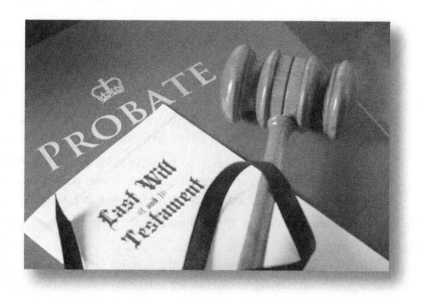

Probate is the judicial process whereby a will is "proved" in a court of law and accepted as a valid public document that is the true last testament of the deceased, or whereby the estate is settled according to the laws of intestacy in the state of residence [or real property] of the deceased at time of death in the absence of a legal will.

In a probate sale, the court will order the real property sold and appoint a real estate agent to sell it.

Over more than 10 years I have handled hundreds of probate estate sales.

Keep in mind that you will be dealing with grieving (and sometimes greedy) family members and these sales can become emotionally taxing if you allow them to. Just remember that you are a neutral third-party assigned to do a job.

With probate, you will work with the attorney, key family members and the appointed trustee to accomplish a successful sale at top dollar.

To dominate in this niche Partner with several family law lawyers or attorneys who specialize in probate in your area and give them copies of your book (Idea #14) that they can hand out to their clients.

In fact, you should consider doing a unique version of your book and placing the attorney on the back cover. Just change out the back cover - it's that simple!

Just like with the Divorce Niche, you can create a version for each attorney you begin working with (the book will be the same inside and only the back cover will change).

Oftentimes in a court ordered probate sale, the judge will assign the real estate agent, and the attorneys you partner with have a lot of pull when it comes to throwing your hat in the ring.

Be sure to create a flyer showcasing your Probate Sale Services.

In addition, if you want to really cement the deal with an attorney you are trying to attract, be sure to interview them for your YouTube channel and Facebook Group (Idea #9).

Chapter Homework

Watch Knolly's FREE Video for this Chapter to help you grow your
success even faster! To watch simply go to
Knolly.com/FreeTMLVideos
or scan the QR Code below to watch.

Videos Included for this Chapter:

☐ **PROBATE: Top 5 Real Estate NICHES in a DOWN
MARKET (PART 4 of 7)**

IDEA #23:
Brand Yourself

BRAND YOURSELF

Remember, your goal is to become famous in the areas that you serve.

To be well known you will have to brand yourself.

This means including your photo and name (or team name) in all of your items of value. In fact, it is recommended that your name, photo and logo make up approximately 30 percent of the marketing piece.

CREATE CONSISTENT AND PURPOSEFUL BRANDING

Entire careers have been built upon the study of consumer behavior as it relates to branding.

Creating a consistent brand across all platforms is critical, if you want to run be a Real Estate Mayor (Idea #8).

Every place that folks see your advertisements and imaging, they should see consistency.

People pay brand managers thousands of dollars to help them create a "Brand Bible".

Here, I'll give you the snapshot version of what folks have paid me big bucks to teach them and what key elements go into your branding:

> **Logo:** create a professional logo and consistently use it across all platforms

> **Slogan:** create a catchy slogan that folks will remember

> **Fonts:** pick a primary font and a secondary font and use them consistently

> **Colors:** pick one or two main complementary colors and use them in all of your marketing.

> **Your Photo:** depending on your industry, it will probably be a good idea to use your photo (and/or logo) as 30% of most of the marketing pieces you create.

Having a face (mascot) for the company really helps folks identify with your business.

There is much more to learn on branding. For a good primer, read *The 22 Immutable Laws of Branding* by Al Ries.

Chapter Homework

Watch Knolly's FREE Video for this Chapter to help you grow your success even faster! To watch simply go to
Knolly.com/FreeTMLVideos
or scan the QR Code below to watch.

Videos Included for this Chapter:

☐ **STOP Chasing Leads! How to Become a Celebrity in Your Marketplace w/Brand Identity MasterClass**

IDEA #24:
Run Targeted
Facebook ADs

One of the best ways to further submit you as the Real Estate Mayor of your area is through the running of Targeted Facebook Ads.

The idea is to only show your Ad to homeowners in the areas you serve, and using Facebook Ads is a great way to do that because you can select exactly who you want to see your ads.

Your ads will simply be **Boosted Posts** from your Facebook Business Page.

These ads can be boosted to folks who live within a small radius of your new listing or the establishment you are interviewing for your YouTube channel.

You can boost Posts that are for Open Houses, Just Solds or Just Listeds or your local business video interviews.

Be sure to deliver your ADS only to:

- Homeowners (folks who own not rent)
- Folks within a small radius of your Open House, Just Sold, Just Listed or video interview.

I have spent tens of thousands of dollars advertising on Facebook and I am consistently pleased with the results and my ability to tweak and specify my target audience.

Since the dynamics of Facebook advertising changes rapidly, I won't get into the specifics here on how to place your Facebook Ads, but be sure to search YouTube and Google to get the most effective strategies for running your Facebook Ad campaigns.

Also, why not ask the establishment you interview if they want to pay to BOOST the post for $50 or $100? For example they can pay $3/day to boost the post for 15 days.

That way you get all your Facebook Ads PAID for!

IDEA #25:
Append Your Tagline to Every Conversation

This idea is extremely powerful, yet it is so simple that it is often overlooked by most real estate agents.

Utilizing this one strategy can get you another one or two leads each month, which could result in an additional 20 or more sales this year!

If your average commission is $6,000 - $9,000, this one strategy could net you six figures!

With every conversation you have always finish it with letting folks know that you are trying to help 2 more families this month and ask them who they know that is looking to buy or sell.

"John, just one more thing. I'm looking to help 2 more families this month. Who do you know that is looking to buy or sell?"

This script should just roll off your tongue like water.

<u>It's the way you should finish every single conversation!</u>

IDEA #26:
Send JUST SOLD
Postcards Around
Your Just Solds

This is an obvious strategy but many agents just simply don't do it.

They either don't believe it works or they don't feel they have the money or time to implore it.

If you want to pick up more listings, you should send JUST LISTED and JUST SOLD postcards around your listings. This will complement the strategies you are utilizing in Idea #7, Idea 8 and Idea #9.

By using Every Door Direct Mail (EDDM) and partnering with local trades (Idea #11), all of your postage and printing costs will be paid for.

IDEA #27:
Partner with We Buy Houses Investors

Over the years I have partnered with many "we buy houses" investors.

These investors are constantly coming across folks who have to sell, but if the numbers don't work and if the homeowner is upside down, they refer them to my team and it's a win-win!

Of course, we also reciprocate by referring them folks who don't want to list and need quick cash to sell.

FINAL THOUGHT:
Only Ever Market for
Seller Listing Leads

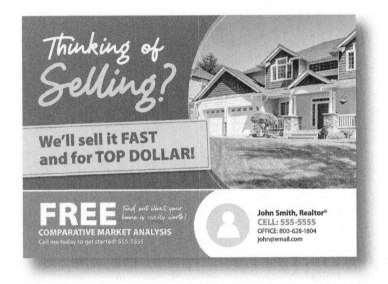

On our final strategy I want to let you in on a POWERFUL idea.

Many are afraid to implement this one!

On our team we never, ever (never) market for anything but seller leads!

I sold more than 1000 houses during my first 10 years in the business and I have never marketed for buyer leads in my career.

All of my marketing has been to generate seller leads (or to market our current listings), and from that marketing my team has had all the buyer leads we can handle.

If you will make this one final idea a principal in your marketing – you will surely see the listings roll in.

Chapter Homework

Watch Knolly's FREE Videos for this Chapter to help you grow your success even faster! To watch simply go to
Knolly.com/FreeTMLVideos
or scan the QR Code below of the videos you want to watch.

Videos Included for this Chapter:

☐ **The 10 Commandments of Lead Generation**

☐ How to LEAD GENERATE Based on Your DISC Personality Profile (MORE LEADS NOW!) (Mentorship Masters)

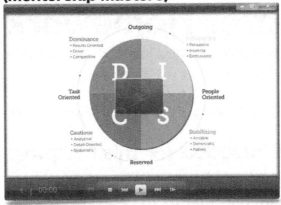

☐ How to Generate a Non-Stop Supply of FREE Leads! Lead Gen Secrets Bonus MasterClass

Knolly's Top 20 Book Recommendations

1. *The Bible (GOD)*

2. *The Power of Your Subconscious Mind* (Dr. Joseph Murphy)

3. *Letting Go: The Pathway to Surrender* (Dr. David Hawkins

4. *The Detox Miracle Sourcebook* (Dr. Robert Morse)

5. *DotCom Secrets* (Russell Brunson)

6. *The Millionaire Real Estate Agent* (Gary Keller)

7. *Success with Listings* (Knolly Williams)

8. *Think and Grow Rick* (Napoleon Hill)

9. *The One Thing* (Gary Keller)

10. *Expert Secrets* (Russell Brunson)

11. *The 4 Hour Workweek* (Tim Ferris)

12. *The 22 Immutable Laws of Branding* (Al Ries & Laura Riles)

13. *The Secret to Permanent Prosperity* (Mike Hernacki)

14. *The Secret to Knowing God's Will for Your Life* (Knolly Williams)

15. *Who Moved My Cheese?* (Spencer Johnson)

16. *Power vs Force* (Dr. David Hawkins)

17. *The 22 Immutable Laws of Marketing* (Al Ries & Jack Trout)

18. *Cure for The Common* Life: Living in Your Sweet Spot (Max *Lucado)*

19. *The Science of Getting Rich* (Wallace D. Wattles)

20. *The E-Myth Revisited (Michael E. Gerber)*

About Knolly...

Knolly Williams is the Founder of Mentorship Masters.

Knolly is an Author, Trainer and National Speaker, and has been featured on ABC, NBC, FOX, CBS, Newsweek and in over 300 newspapers worldwide.

Using the ancient wisdom found in the Bible, Knolly has coached tens of thousands of real estate agents, entrepreneurs, business owners and individuals on how to become all that God created them to be, so that they can live the life they were meant to live.

Knolly has been a business owner and an entrepreneur since the age of 13, and he has launched multiple 6 and 7 figure businesses over the years.

In 1992 at the age of 22, Knolly launched his first business (a Christian Record Label). With just $1,800 in startup capital which he raised from family and friends. The Lord blessed his efforts, and the company grew to a seven-figure business, becoming the #1 Record Label in its genre in the world, with 14 employees and 18 recording artists.

After 10 successful years, the music industry tanked and Knolly and his wife Josie lost everything including an elegant 6,000 square foot home, executive office building, private recording studio and 10-acre paradise just outside Austin, TX.

After some deep soul searching, Knolly was led into the real estate industry.

In 2003, at the age of 33 Knolly started over at rock bottom. The Lord once again blessed his endeavors.

Knolly grew to become one of the top 7 real estate agents in Austin, TX (ranked by Austin Business Journal out of more than 9,500 agents and based on actual production).

Knolly sold more than 1000 homes during his first 10 years in the business, placing him within the top 1% of REALTORS® in the United States.

Knolly now teaches, trains and equips real estate agents with the training, mentorship and coaching they need to thrive at the highest levels!

Mentorship Masters, which commands the majority of Knolly's focus is the fulfillment of Knolly's lifelong dream to provide no-cost training and mentorship to real estate agents around the world.

You can join for FREE at PartnerWithKnolly.com

ALSO AVAILABLE:

Knolly's National Bestseller: *SUCCESS WITH LISTINGS*

Made in the USA
Coppell, TX
25 March 2022

75528216R00085